Sociology for Schools

Jane L. Thompson

Sociology for Schools
Book 1

Hutchinson Educational

HUTCHINSON EDUCATIONAL LTD
3 Fitzroy Square, London W1

London Melbourne Sydney Auckland
Wellington Johannesburg Cape Town
and agencies throughout the world

First published 1973
Second impression 1974

© Jane L. Thompson 1973

This book has been set in Times type, printed in Great Britain
on smooth wove paper by Anchor Press, and
bound by Wm. Brendon, both of Tiptree, Essex

ISBN 0 09 114251 2

Contents

Contents

Part One

Introduction to Sociology

Chapter 1

Individual and Group

Each Person is an Individual

If you look around the classroom you're sitting in, you'll see a group of pupils, the same people you see every day and who by now you probably take for granted. They are always there; looking the same as usual, behaving in much the same way as they always behave.

If instead of pupils, however, you found yourself sitting next to a hippy dressed in caftan and beads, or a Borstal boy sitting in his prison uniform, or a girl in a raggy dress with a black eye and a bruised face, then you would surely take more notice of them. If instead of the teacher who is talking to you at the front of the room, you saw a dreamy young lady strumming a guitar and singing to herself, or a man dressed up in frog-man's gear, then here again you would sit up just a little straighter and show a little more interest.

What you would be seeing in fact would be a group of individuals – different people with different appearances, interests, attitudes and behaviour.

Now look again at the pupils you know well and see every day. They are individuals too. Each one is playing the part of a pupil at this moment, but each one is nevertheless different in his own way. Each is made up of a mixture of the abilities he was born with and the qualities he has learned since the second he drew breath. No one individual in your class is like any other.

This is true of society as a whole. Society is made up of many individuals, each of whom is unique in his own right. Of course, no one individual can exist alone – part of the fact of living in societies means we are all social beings and therefore need the support and company of other social beings to survive. We shall go on to see how individuals join together with others of a similar type to form groups within society and how within these groups, identifying features, behaviour, attitudes, and patterns of life become much the same. But before we look at group behaviour, let us return to a consideration of individual behaviour and see just what it is that makes the individual behave socially as he does.

Individual Characteristics

If you were describing a school friend that you know very well as accurately as you could in an attempt to show what sort of person he or she is, these are the factors that you would have to take into account:

Appearance
who he/she takes
after in looks

Personality and
Behaviour

Family and
Background
where he/she lives
parents
brothers and sisters
feelings about family

Leisure
Activities and
Interests

How he/she is
treated by others
e.g. parents, teachers,
school-friends

Background and Upbringing

The type of family and background a child comes from affects his behaviour very much. Consider together these examples:

(i) When a couple are married for a long time before they have a child, his mother could well be forty when the child is born, and his father perhaps forty-five. An only child brought up by parents who have long been childless could well be spoiled, and too restricted to adult company. As he grows older, this could make the child's relationship with other youngsters difficult.

When he becomes a teenager, say fifteen, his parents will seem almost like old people and he may find it difficult to talk to them about his hopes and fears.

(ii) Identical twins will most likely have a childhood in which they are dressed exactly the same and continually mistaken for each other. This may be fun but it also means that it is difficult for them to establish their own individual personalities and they must therefore be resigned to always being considered exactly like someone else.

Twins will probably have strong emotional ties to each other, however, but this could make separation, in schools for example, very upsetting.

(iii) A child whose mother dies when he is very small is left with only one parent. Since many fathers find difficulty in bringing up children and looking after a house without a wife to help them, neighbours and relatives will be called in to lend a hand. The child will probably miss the care and guidance a mother can give and may feel confused and afraid of his difference from other children.

If the child is a girl, it is likely that as she grows older she will be expected to take on the 'housewife's role' and look after her father, the house and other children.

If the father marries again, the children will have to adapt themselves to a new stepmother whom they did not choose and whom they may not like very much, if at all.

Discussion and Written Work

1 (a) Make a copy of the chart on p. 12 in your book. Choose a friend to describe and make notes about him/her in the spaces on your chart.
(b) Write a character study of your friend using the above information.

2 Here are some examples of different pupils' personality and behaviour. In each case write a piece to explain how their background or upbringing could have caused them to be like this:
(a) Very shy and frightened of grown men
(b) Very cheeky to teachers
(c) Mean – never willing to lend or share their possessions
(d) Big-headed and inclined to show off
(e) Quiet and hard-working in school
(f) Always trying to get the sympathy or attention of teachers
(g) A bit serious and 'old-fashioned' in ideas and interests
(h) Always noisy and inclined to shout in a loud voice

3 Imagine that at the age of three weeks you were adopted by the Queen. Write an essay to describe yourself as you would now be, having grown up in the Royal Family.

You should comment on your behaviour in relation to the following:
(a) Dress
(b) Language
(c) Relationships with your adopted parents
(d) Schooling – education
(e) Interests and leisure-time activities
(f) Friends
(g) Responsibilities
(h) Job opportunities
(i) Social pressures on you (the ways you would be expected to behave by others)

4 Imagine that either Prince Charles or Princess Anne had been adopted into your family at the age of three weeks.
Using the same headings (a–i above), show how his or her behaviour would have developed under these circumstances.

5 Suggest how your personality and behaviour might have developed if you had been brought up in one of the following situations:
(a) Reared by Gypsies
(b) Adopted by a very famous film star who spent a lot of time travelling abroad making films
(c) Brought up in a very large family by adults who had not enough money to make ends meet
(d) Brought up by a family living in Russia
(e) Brought up by someone who was a successful lawyer

6 *A Negro Girl from Alabama*
(The Negro girl takes an English reporter to the graveyard where many of her relatives are buried, and in telling him the causes of their deaths, gives a powerful insight into her background and upbringing.)

We made the woods and the little Negro graveyard she wanted to show me because so many of her relatives were buried there. She wanted to show me her family history; she seemed to think Englishmen attached great importance to family histories. Her eldest sister who had been 'a saint' was buried there. So was her uncle who had been badly wounded in the Second World War – I was tempted to write 'the War' because, to my generation of Englishmen, there is only one war, but in the Deep South, 'the War' so often means the Civil War which in so many ways is still being decided. There was a grandfather who had been lynched – he was supposed to have made a pass at a white woman ('She was so ugly nobody anywhere had ever made a pass at her and my grand-daddy was the best looking man in this part of the country'). There was a simple black cross for a nephew who had disappeared after he had stood up to a local white farmer ('There was a knock one night, he went to the door, and he was never seen again. Bodies, cut up, unrecognizable, often turn up in the swamp or the river'). She told a story, a local story, as if one of the graves reminded her of it. A local white farmer took a fancy to a local Negro girl. He didn't want to marry her of course; just sleep with her every now and then. So she and her Negro boy friend went to the next town to get married and, so they hoped, avoid trouble. But when they came back and the white man sought her again and she showed him the wedding ring, he killed the boy – her husband – and then he killed her, and then he killed her parents. 'It was a long time ago, but things haven't changed that much,' she said. When she was a young girl she saw an aunt – 'the pretty one' – raped by a local white man. . . .

'Are your parents buried here?' I asked, trying to divert her from the blood stories. But she was set in the mood now. She was the teacher, giving me a digest of Negro history through the ages. She told me the story of a slave who had twice escaped and how, the second time they caught him, his master poured hot lard over him and, when some of the other slave owners had protested, how he explained that the slave had been 'incorrigible'. . . .

Her parents weren't dead, she said unwillingly. Her father was somewhere up North. Her mother was in Florida. She was ready to leave. It was much later that I learnt her parents hadn't been married, that her mother had eight children, each by a different man and had been in hospital for taking drugs. She had last seen her father when she was five. Her mother came and went in her life, and she spoke of her with a mixture of love and hatred. Her parents were her burden: she saw herself repeating their lives, all the failure she saw in them; this fear was a constant pressure and drove her into acts of denial.

From *Breaking the Silence* by W. J. Weatherby

(a) Explain what happened to the girl's grandfather and nephew. How does she feel about these two deaths?

(b) Give two examples from the passage to show how white men frequently take advantage of Negro women.

(c) Why was the girl unwilling to say much about her parents?

(d) From what you have discovered about the girl's family background, write a piece to describe what you think her attitudes to life and people are likely to be.

Social Roles

A person's behaviour varies depending on the type of situation he finds himself in and the type of people he is in contact with. Discuss together these examples:

(i) If you had to go to the funeral of a very close relative, your behaviour in this situation would be very different from what it would be if you went to a friend's birthday party.

(ii) If you were talking to your friends about what you did in your spare time, it would be a very different conversation from the one with the head-teacher when you were called into his/her room to explain why you had not done your homework.

The parts played by people in their daily life we call their social roles.

Role Conflict

As we understand the individual more clearly, it becomes evident that he is playing not just one social role, but many. You are not only a pupil, but also a son or daughter, a friend, a grandchild, a footballer or pop fan, a babysitter or an errand-boy. If you made a list of your social roles you would probably want to add many more to these. Some roles are contra-dictory, and frequently, when they contradict, the individual can find himself in a state of role conflict.

Here are some examples to discuss:

(i) If you are a good pupil, you realise the need to work hard, to do your homework, and to please your teachers. If you are a good son or daughter, you feel you ought to help out at home, perhaps by doing a little house-work, or by looking after the younger ones while your parents go out. If you are a good friend, it is likely that your pals will arrive on your doorstep in the evening and insist that you come and join them. Here is a role con-flict – which role do you play? That of conscientious pupil? That of dependable son or daughter? That of a popular friend?

(ii) If a woman is interested and keen to continue her career after she gets married, she is likely to meet with a role conflict, especially if a child is born. Does she still give her time and enthusiasm to her work? Or does she give up her job to provide a good and secure home for her husband and family?

(iii) In the process of investigating some vandalism on a new estate, a policeman finds that his own son is one of the principal offenders. Here is a conflict between the role of policeman and the role of father. Does he treat the boy in the same way as the rest of the gang and charge him according to the law? Or does he allow his feelings as a father to let him overlook his son's part in the trouble? Or does he let all the boys go?

Discussion and Written Work

1 (a) Describe how you would be expected to behave at the funeral of a close relative.

(b) Describe how you would be likely to behave at the birthday party of a friend.

(c) Write a conversation between you and your friend in which you tell him or her about what you did the previous evening.

(d) Write the conversation between you and the headteacher in which you try to excuse yourself for not doing your homework the previous evening.

(e) Give an example from your own experience to show how your behaviour has been very different in two differing situations.

2 Write an account of the role of two of the following people:
(a) footballer (b) pop star (c) teenager (d) grandmother (e) champion athlete (f) housewife

You should try to show the typical behaviour of each of the people chosen by which their roles can be identified. It would be a good idea to begin by copying down these headings and by making notes against each before turning these notes into a proper essay.

(i)   *Appearance* (how they could be identified)
(ii)   *Age Group*
(iii) *Characteristic Behaviour*
(iv)   *Characteristic Attitudes*
(v)   *The Way in which the Role has been Learned*
(vi)   *Relationships with Others*
(vii) *Effects on Others*

Try to find pictures which could be the very people whose roles you have described, and mount them in your book.

3 Give two examples from your own knowledge or experience to illustrate a role conflict situation. In each case describe carefully the way in which two sets of expectations clash with each other to cause the conflict.

4 Mr Jones is a teacher. He has spent a long time building up a good relationship with two very difficult boys who are always in trouble at school and are therefore disliked by the rest of the staff. In an attempt to get to know them, Mr Jones spends some of his spare time with the boys. On one occasion they go to a café and put some money in the juke box. Here is his account of the role conflict he found himself in:

'Now all at once, I found myself in a difficult position, for the juke box was

17

going wrong, and apart from playing the requested records, was disgorging sixpences and shillings at a fairly rapid rate. The boys were naturally delighted! As a result I found myself in the middle of a robbery of the juke box and my most advisable course of action was by no means clear. It *was* clear that the correct moral action would have set me well apart from them and detracted, to some extent, from the progress we had made during the past few weeks. I therefore took the 'Aren't we lucky' approach, which must have sounded pretty lame but I was not keen to discourage them too actively. All this time of course I was desperately hoping that the flow of cash would cease, which it did quite soon. The boys then split the haul and we went back to my flat.'
From *Young Teachers and Reluctant Learners*, by Hannam, Stephenson and Smyth

(a) Why were the boys delighted when the juke box went wrong?
(b) What did the boys intend to do with the money?
(c) There were two courses of action open to Mr Jones. Describe each of them and explain the possible advantages and disadvantages of each.
(d) Which course did Mr Jones take?
(e) Explain carefully with reasons why you think his decision was either the right one or the wrong one
(f) Explain why the above incident created a role conflict for Mr Jones

Social Groups
Although Society is made up of individuals, these individuals need to have relationships of various kinds with other individuals.

When a number of individuals who have similar interests or attitudes, or a common point of contact, combine together for a certain purpose, then a group is formed.

To be a part of a group it is necessary for the collection of people described to be involved together in social contact for a period of time.

As individuals, we belong to many groups; some, such as the family, last for life; others, such as a sports team, or a group of workers in the same firm, or a Darby and Joan Club, last only for a phase of our life.

How many different groups do you belong to? Three which apply to all of you are the family, the pupils of your school, and teenagers.

What Makes a Group?
Members of the same group can always be recognised because they have several important things in common. This can best be shown by a simple diagram.

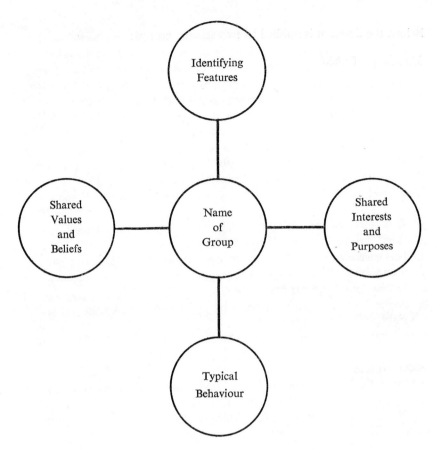

Each group is made up of the following common factors:
(a) A Name
(b) Identifying Features (e.g. age, sex, uniform, meeting place, etc.)
(c) Typical Behaviour
(d) Shared Interests and Purpose (the common concern or reason for contact)
(e) Shared Values and Beliefs (common attitudes and ways of reacting)

Below, the diagram is applied to two specific groups:

Manchester United

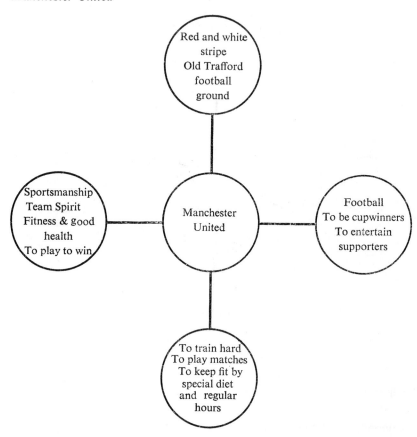

Skinheads

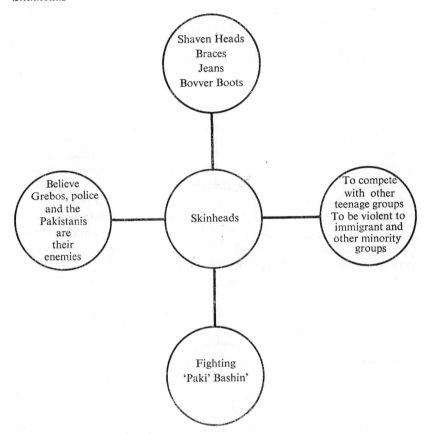

Conformity and Group Norms

If you were involved in an important football match, perhaps the local schools cup final, your chances of winning would soon be wrecked if the centre-forward decided to go to the pictures for the afternoon, or if the inside-left turned up to play in his mountaineering outfit. On occasions like this, every member of the group has to do what he is supposed to do if the group is to be able to hold together.

This is true of all group behaviour. If everyone in the group decided 'to do his own thing', regardless of the rest, the results would be chaotic. Imagine what would happen if everyone arrived at school at different times, or if a large number of parents decided that bringing up children was not their responsibility and so left them to fend for themselves. If there was no government and no laws and people were allowed to do exactly what they liked, when they liked, the society would soon break

21

down. If societies are to be able to survive without too much disruption, then it is important to make sure that their members accept general patterns of behaviour and agree to conform to them.

Most groups also demand that their members behave in a certain way with the result that groups can be recognised by their typical behaviour, attitudes, customs and habits. Members of a group have to conform to this characteristic behaviour or to what is called the norms of the group.

The norms of a group are not set down by law or enforced by fines and imprisonment, but they are backed by tradition, expectation, and habit so that it becomes the accepted thing for people to comply with them.

In some families, for example, the norms are that the father may well make all the decisions and his wife will be expected to agree. It will be his job to pay the bills, tend to the garden, change plugs, and organise the decorating. His wife may well see to the clothing and kitting out of the children, cook the meals, and do the housework. The children may go to bed at a set time, take turns with the washing up, be responsible for cleaning their own rooms, and feeding the pets. The norms of each family will vary depending on the shared attitudes of its members.

In a youth club, the norms will be those of being a typical 'trendy' teenager who is fashionable, likes pop music and dancing, takes an interest in the sport and activities of the club, and who likes to mix with other young people of similar tastes.

Why Conform?
People usually conform to group norms because they like to be well thought of by their fellows. They like to be 'one of the gang' or 'one of the boys', and to be included in all the activities of the group.

When someone goes against the norms of the group, he soon finds himself out of favour and even in a position of isolation. The 'teacher's pet' who is always telling tales or working too hard, goes against the class group norms of 'conspiracy' against the staff and 'skiving' homework. The youth club member who damages property, or starts a fight, goes against the group norms of having a good time in a friendly and social atmosphere. The blackleg who refuses to stop work goes against the group norms of the strikers who want to withdraw their labour.

In this sort of situation, the group can exert several sanctions against, or withdrawal of privileges from, renegade members who don't conform. Children often make fun of the odd child out, such as the fat boy who isn't good at games, or the 'swot' who shows them up by working too enthusiastically. Some adults will send individuals 'to Coventry', which means that they will refuse to speak to them. Some will be made to feel so unwelcome that they will have no alternative but to leave the group. Many of the people in society whom we call 'drop outs' have in fact been forced out of established groups because they refused to conform to the group norms.

Social Pressure

On the whole, however, people seem to need to be respected and to be well thought of by other people in their groups. So much so that many are frightened to speak out against the views of the majority or take an individual stand on something controversial. Because of this people can be easily swayed or easily persuaded to act in a conformist way, and it takes the brave man to reject what the majority of his fellows are taking for granted. When an individual is forced into behaving in a certain way to gain the approval of his group, we call this process social pressure. The group or society decides by mutual agreement what is acceptable behaviour and then proceeds to exert influence on individual members to comply.

Discussion and Written Work

1 (a) Write down the groups in the following list which apply to you: pop fan group; sports team; scouts; guides; youth clubs; street gang; soccer fans; church; school choir.
(b) What other groups do you belong to?
(c) Make a list of the groups your parents belong to.
(d) What groups do you belong to in common with your parents? Why?
(e) List the different groups your parents belong to. Why do these particular groups differ from yours?

2 Construct group diagrams similar to those on p. 19–21 to show the characteristic features of the following groups: (a) a pop group (b) a family (c) policemen (d) teachers (e) politicians (f) dockers (g) soldiers (h) school pupils.

3 Write a piece describing and explaining the norms of your class group. State clearly what you expect of each other and how you usually behave. Explain how far your expectations of each other agree with those held by the teachers who teach you. Is 'a good member of the class' in your opinion the same as 'a good member of the class' in the teacher's opinion? Why?

4 (a) Why do we refer to some teenagers as drop outs?
(b) How would you recognise or describe them?
(c) Explain some of their reasons for dropping out.

5 (a) Tramps have also been called drop outs. Explain clearly the sorts of reasons that cause them to behave in the way they do.

(b) What are the main differences between the way of life of a tramp and that of a typical married man in a family like your own, or that of someone you know well?

6 Read carefully the following quotations, then do the work which follows:

(a) In films, beautiful girls in tortoiseshell spectacles and flat heeled shoes are first humiliated for competing with men, then they are forgiven, loved, and allowed to be glamorous only when they admit their error.

From *Male and Female*, by Margaret Mead

(a) What sort of social pressure is Margaret Mead talking about here?
(b) What are the commonly held expectations about women in our society which make them subject to this kind of pressure?

(b) I've become a public and professional Flower Person – but my private life's another matter. I've got the responsibility of a wife and family.

Tony Burrows of the Flowerpot Men pop group

(a) Tony Burrows' public image is that of a Flower Person. What are the characteristics of a Flower Person?
(b) How do social pressures prevent Tony Burrows carrying this image through into his private life?
(c) What is your opinion of Tony Burrows' dual role?

(c) Everytime I get in late, my Dad's waiting up for me and he goes mad and smells my breath. But the lads would all think that I was a kid or a 'mummy's boy' if I left the club any earlier. I don't want to look stupid.

Tom, age 15

(a) Explain carefully why Tom is in a state of role conflict.
(b) What social pressures do his friends put upon him?
(c) Suggest another two examples to show how friends of the same age can exert social pressure on individuals.

7 Study the extracts carefully, then attempt the written work:

MANUEL
(Manuel remembers how at the age of 13 he was a member of the Casa Grande gang.)

24

Alberto and I were members of the Casa Grande gang. There were about forty of us then; we played games, like burro, or told dirty jokes together, and we were always very proud of keeping up the name of the Casa Grande. The guys from the streets of the Barbers, the Painters, or the Tinsmiths could never get the better of us. At dances we kept our eyes peeled to see that they didn't hang around trying to make the girls of the Casa Grande.

Every sixteenth of September a certain gang would come with sticks to make war against us. We would let them come in through one of the gates, and, meanwhile, the Janitor's son, who was a member of our gang, would lock the other gate. When all of the gang was inside, he would run and lock the first gate. Then we would let them have it in all the courtyards, with stones, pails of water, and sticks.

We never let anyone get the better of us. Alberto and I were the first to take on any others . . . we were known as good fighters and were always put up front against other gangs. We fought so much in those days, I began to dream about it. . .

All during my boyhood, and even afterwards, I spent a lot of time with my gang. We had no chief or leader . . . he would have to be too good at everything . . . but some boys were outstanding in one way or another. We didn't have bad characters like some gangs. There was one bunch in our neighbourhood that was known for stealing money from drunks, and for taking marijuana. Only one boy in my gang took to the needle and went bad. In my day, we never did anything worse than grab the girls by their behinds . . . things like that. . .

At that time I very much admired my older cousin, Salvador, the only child of my aunt Guadalupe. He was the terror of the gang of the Street of the Bakers, a really tough gang; of all the members he was the one that was most feared. But I admired him only because he was a good fighter. Otherwise, I didn't think much of him because of the nasty way in which he spoke to my aunt, especially when he was drunk.

From *Children of Sanchez*, by Oscar Lewis

(a) What is a gang?

(b) What 'point of contact' decided which particular gang a boy should belong to?

(c) Explain with reference to the passage what types of behaviour were highly respected by Manuel's gang.

(d) What types of behaviour did Manuel's gang look down upon?

(e) How are the norms of Manuel's gang illustrated by his attitude to Salvador?

(f) Do you belong, or have you ever belonged, to a gang? What was the 'point of contact' which brought you together?

(g) Write a short account of the kinds of behaviour and attitudes which are typical of your gang.

(h) Do you have a member of the gang whom everyone more or less accepts as leader? Why is this?

MARTA

When I was about twelve, I began to take account of things and stopped playing with boys. I liked to dress up and I changed my clothes every day. Consuelo was doing my washing and ironing then, and was annoyed. So I had to learn to half wash things myself. I spent my pennies on ribbons and adornments and pasted beauty marks on my face. For a long time, I wore an artificial carnation in my hair thinking it made me look pretty, even though it was torn and spotted and the wire stem showed. My father seemed to enjoy seeing me fix myself up like that.

Once I got into a fight with a girl who pulled off my beauty mark. I was so mad I tore her dress from top to bottom, as though it had been cut with a scissors. I was always getting into fights because some girls are vipers; they get jealous, tell lies about each other, and start trouble.

I fought with boys too. If they said or did anything to me, I never let them get away with it. One fellow who was bigger than I, tripped me when I was running around the courtyard. I fell and cracked my head. I wasn't scared, just very angry, and when my head was better I went after him for revenge. I hit him so much, his mother complained to my *papa*. But father didn't pay any attention to her.

My best friends were Irela and Ema, the daughter of Enoe. Chita was also my friend, but not so much as the others. We had all grown up together and defended each other tooth and nail. If one was treated badly by her family, the others invited her to go home with them. If one ate, the others ate, even if it were only beans. I placed all my confidence in these girls and we did everything together.

La Chata had the habit of sending me to the *pulqueria* every day, for a bottle of *pulque* to drink with her dinner. She did it secretly, because my *papa* had forbidden us to go to such places. One day, I had the idea of buying an extra bottle for me and my friends. We went up to the roof where no-one could see us drink it. After that, we bought a small bottle of *tequila* every Sunday and finished it off together on the roof. There were times when we were so drunk, we couldn't climb down the ladder. If I didn't know how to control myself, I would have got the drinking habit, like Irela and Ema.

We smoked on the roof too, and told dirty stories. Then we would go and buy chewing gum to take away the odour of the nicotine. Irela and Ema would steal – once they stole money from the school bank – but I never joined them. I just didn't have that desire for extra money or things. I had enough spending money because during school vacations my father let me work in an ice-cream factory near my house. They paid me two or three pesos a day and I spent it all on myself. My father never asked me for the money I earned. With it I bought what I pleased, socks, sweets, clothing . . . but most of my money went to rent a bicycle or to go to the swimming pool with my friends.

From *Children of Sanchez*, by Oscar Lewis

(a) When Marta was about 12 she wanted to be more grown up. Give as many examples from the passage as you can to illustrate this.

(b) But she was not altogether 'ladylike'. Give two examples to show that she was still a bit of a 'tomboy'.

(c) What was the 'point of contact' which drew Marta and her friends together into a group?

(d) Give five examples of the group behaviour that the girls shared.

(e) In what way did Marta still retain some of her individuality in the group?

Chapter 2

Social Class

Social Stratification

If you were to look at a diagram of the cross-section of a mountain you would see several layers of different kinds of rock resting one upon the other. These layers are called rock strata.

The same sort of diagram of society would look like a pyramid divided into layers. At the top of the pyramid would be the minority of people in society who have the greatest amount of wealth, power and prestige. Further down would be various wider layers of people with less wealth, power and prestige. At the bottom of the pyramid would be the majority of people, who have the least wealth, power and prestige in society.

There is no society known to man in which the individual members are all completely equal to each other. In every case some form of social stratification takes place, that is, the arrangement of groups in society into higher and lower levels judged in terms of their wealth, power and prestige.

Stratification and Social Class

Stratification in Britain is based on social class and the classes are arranged hierarchically (most influential first, least influential last) like this:

Upper Class (hereditary aristocracy, large property owners)
Upper Middle Class (wealthy businessmen, property owners, professional, and managerial occupations)
Lower Middle Class (lesser professional, small business interests, minor supervisory, white collar)
Upper Working Class (clerical, skilled trades)
Lower Working Class (semi-skilled, unskilled and manual occupations)

In the past it was possible to identify a person's social class by the amount of money he possessed. But this is no longer adequate. For example, a docker can earn a minimum of £2,000 a year while a school teacher may earn slightly more than half of that. The school teacher, however, is of a higher social class than the docker.

To determine the social class of an individual today, the sociologist would take the following factors into account:

(i) Amount of money earned and wealth possessed

(ii) Type of job and the status that goes with it
(iii) Degree of influence and power over other people implied by the job
(iv) Education
(v) Style of living
(vi) Attitudes to life

By using these factors to group people together into social classes, sociologists have found that each social class tends to have a different way of life, different customs, values and standards, and a different set of expectations and aspirations. Children born into a particular social class learn the type of behaviour typical of their class and can be identified by it.

Social Mobility

While a child is born into the social class of its parents and in many cases retains the same social class all its life, it is increasingly possible for children to alter the level of their original class by their own efforts during their lifetime. This movement is called social mobility. While you may occasionally hear of a wealthy man losing all his fortune and being forced to live in much humbler circumstances, the movement is mostly from a lower to a higher level.

The opportunity for the individual to improve the level of his social class comes largely through education. For example, a working class boy could go to university, qualify as a lawyer or doctor, and thus move up in the social scale.

A second way is by marriage. A working class girl could marry a bank clerk with high social and work ambitions and she would then move with him into the lower middle class.

A third way is by increased wealth. This could mean an improved standard of living and the acquisition of the trappings of middle class life that go with it, although the attitudes and values of the middle classes cannot be acquired merely by increased wealth.

Status

A person's status in society is very much tied to his social class and depends to a great extent upon how he is viewed in the eyes of others. People of a higher class tend to have a higher social status because of the prestige that goes with their jobs. For example, doctor, lawyer, businessman, and teacher are more respected occupations in social terms than labourer, factory worker, dustman or docker. Even though each occupation is of vital importance to society and many people would like to see each respected equally for the differing contributions he makes, this distinction in status is very strongly felt by society as a whole.

Power

Power also usually belongs to the higher social classes because their wealth, education and type of occupation gives them the opportunity to exert more influence on the running of the country than members of the lower class. One contradiction to this generalisation, however, is the power of some organised trades unions to exercise considerable influence on policy decisions because of their threat to strike.

Speech

It has been shown by sociologists that while everyone in Britain speaks the same language, there are in fact two forms of this language. One is the informal, everyday, short-sentenced, slangy language that we use among people we know very well. This kind of language is simple. The sentences are frequently unfinished, or trail off, in comments like, 'you know', 'isn't it', 'you see', and 'wouldn't it', which allow the speaker to be brief and not to explain himself more fully.

The other is the more complicated, long-worded, intricate-sentenced language that is used in more formal situations. On the whole middle class people can use both types of language while working class people only ever use the first type. This means that middle class people frequently appear more intelligent and more informed than the working class. The ability to use a more complicated language also means that middle class children find it easier to study and to do better in school subjects than working class children.

Also, if you consider a person's accent, it is usually the case that the more middle class a person is, the less apparent is his accent, while working class people usually use a more noticeably strong local accent.

Dress and Appearance

If you are standing in a cinema queue, it is often possible to say which social class the other individuals in the queue belong to by their dress and appearance. While everyone tends to follow the latest fashions, there is a considerable difference in quality between those bought expensively by the middle class from rather exclusive shops and tailors and those bought cheaply by the working class from chain stores and catalogues.

The working class living on a weekly income are unlikely to buy a whole outfit of clothes at one time. Chiefly because of this their colours and styles do not always match very well. Also, working class people without much extra money to spend do not usually think in terms of buying expensive clothes. Even if they have a 'windfall', the children or the house are 'treated' first.

Middle class people can afford to spend more on clothes and they give high priority to quality, style and neatness. Middle class ladies are far less likely than the working class to be caught without their make-up or in their curlers by unexpected visitors, or to go out shopping like this.

If you watched the various classes going off to work, the appearance of the man destined for the office would be much different to that of the labourer in donkey jacket and overalls with dirt-engrained hands making for the building site. The working class mother doing a part-time job in a factory to make a little extra money, while bringing up several young children in a council house on a low income, would look very different to the middle-class lady who helps the W.V.S. two mornings a week while her cleaning woman sorts out the more tiresome aspects of the housework.

Behaviour and Attitudes

People's behaviour and attitudes to life are considerably affected by the type of work they do. A good education will secure a high status job, which will in turn imply a 'nice house in the suburbs', well-mannered children brought up with respect for adults and property, a willingness to defer present satisfaction for future ambitions, and leisure activities that are quietly social, shared with people of the same class.

A secondary education cut short at 16, followed by lower status employment, will most likely mean a council house on an estate or a rented house in the older area of the city. Parents will be less ambitious for their children, who will be encouraged to live for the present, earn their own living as soon as they can, and enjoy themselves while they are young. Leisure activities will revolve around the family and the neighbourhood, and will most likely be more rowdy and outward-going than those of the middle classes.

Life Styles

In any generalisation there are obviously exceptions to the rule, but if we were to compare the life-styles of middle class people and working class people, it would be possible to make the following *generalisations* about their typical characteristics:

The middle class are more likely than the working class to:
(i) go to church
(ii) go to university
(iii) go abroad for their holidays
(iv) live in their own house in the suburbs
(v) drink privately and play more expensive sports (golf, tennis)
(vi) have professional jobs such as lawyers, doctors, teachers, bankers
(vii) go to 'cocktail parties'

(viii) value education for their children

(ix) read newspapers like The Times, Telegraph, Guardian

(x) be better informed about news and politics

(xi) use a more complex form of language

(xii) plan for the future and defer present satisfaction for ultimate goals

The working class are more likely than the middle class to:

(i) live in council houses or poor quality houses lacking basic amenities

(ii) live very close to their families and relatives

(iii) be in trouble with the police

(iv) leave school at 16

(v) change jobs frequently

(vi) buy goods on hire purchase

(vii) watch I.T.V. rather than B.B.C.

(viii) be less informed about the world and how the state systems of organisation work

(ix) live for the present, and prefer immediate satisfactions to planning far ahead

(x) undervalue education for their children

Discussion and Written Work

1 THE PAINS OF 'MOVING UP'

When a working class girl passes her scholarship for the city grammar school, she must often endure the scorn of other working class children:

When I got to Ash Grange and wore the uniform, the other children used to shout about that. I didn't mind so much. I felt superior. But I had a violin as well, and I used to dread carrying that violin case. I used to plot my way from the yard at home to the teachers, but that violin case seemed to stand out – that brought more bashings than anything else.

From *Education and the Working Class*, by Jackson and Marsden

(a) Why did the other children make fun of the girl's uniform?

(b) Why was she proud of her school uniform?

(c) Why do you think the violin case was such a symbol of ridicule?

(d) How do you think the middle class girls at school reacted to the girl from a working class home?

2 LIVING CONDITIONS

The range of housing among the middle-class families was very great – from a large detached house with six bedrooms, a nursery, study, dining-room, two bathrooms, etc., in three-quarters of an acre of grounds in one of the most fashionable areas of London to a small flat above a shop in a busy high street. But 71 per cent lived in houses which they either owned already or were in the process of purchasing by mortgage. 87 per cent of these houses were in small suburban roads, with an average of three bedrooms, one or two living rooms and a small garden. 21 per cent of the families lived in flats, some of these very modern and elegant, but all the families living in flats intended at some point to move to a house. 'I like a flat, but when you've got children – well a house is more convenient,' was a typical comment, as was the remark that it's 'always better to pay for something you're going to own yourself'. 8 per cent of the families lived in 'working-class style', that is in rooms without a separate entrance in a converted house. One family was lucky in having its own lavatory and bath-room, but the others faced the conditions so common among working-class families, of sharing lavatories, and managing without bathrooms. All of them had every intention of moving, and two had already set in motion the process of buying a house, though in both cases it meant moving out of London into the country in order to do so. None of the middle-class families were tenants of the Council. The position of the working class in this survey was entirely dif-ferent. 4 per cent of the families lived in terraced houses which they owned and 2 per cent of the families rented an entire house from the Council. 6 per cent lived in private blocks of flats, and 17 per cent in Council blocks. The majority, that is 71 per cent, of the families lived in rooms. 87 per cent of these were in small Victorian houses which had been divided up in recent years to house an average of three of four families. For those who were lucky enough to have had their landlords bought out by the Council – 25 per cent – things were not too bad as the Council was committed either to rehousing them or to modern-izing their existing accommodation. The conditions of those living in privately rented accommodation were noticeably lower than that of any other group. One of the worst off was the wife of a labourer who lived with her husband and twin sons of nine months in one room in which they cooked, ate, slept, and spent their leisure. There was no bathroom and the lavatory was shared with all the other occupants of the house, numbering to about ten. For this they paid £3 per week. 42 per cent of the families lived in two rooms, one of which served as a kitchen, living room and sometimes as a bedroom as well. For parents and children to sleep in the same room was commonplace. 71 per cent of the families in rooms had no bathroom. 48 per cent of them were sharing their lavatory with at least one other family, and in one case, the family lived over a small factory and had to share the lavatory during the day with fifteen men employed in the factory. 53 per cent of these families were without a bath and shared their lavatory. All but three of them were tenants of private landlords. Rents varied from 16s. to £5 and among those living in privately owned rooms there seemed no relationship between rent and facilities offered. Thus one family living in two

B

rooms without a bathroom and sharing a lavatory were paying 19s. 6d. The great majority were extremely keen to move, though for most moving was more a dream than a possibility. Like their middle-class counterparts many working-class mothers dreamt of a house. 'I'd move tomorrow if we could find something', said the wife who lived over the factory, 'but we're tied because if we move my husband loses his job'. 'We're saving like mad to put seven hundred down on a house', said the wife of a motor mechanic, 'but it's got to be a New Town: there's no hope for people like us in London'.

From *The Captive Wife*, by Hannah Gavron

(a) What percentage of the middle class either owned or were buying their own houses?

(b) (i) What percentage of the working class owned their own houses?
    (ii) What type of houses did they own?

(c) What percentage of the middle class lived in small suburban roads?

(d) Explain carefully how the majority of the working class lived.

(e) What were the living conditions and future prospects like for those working class families living in Council property?

(f) Give two examples from the passage to illustrate the lower standards of living conditions endured by those working class families in privately rented property.

(g) Why was there no uniformity in the rents of private property?

(h) What percentage of those living in rooms lacked the basic amenities of bathroom and private lavatory?

(i) (i) What percentage of the middle class lived in flats?
    (ii) What were their flats like and what attitude did they have to flat dwelling?

(j) What percentage of the working class lived in flats?

(k) (i) What percentage of the middle class lived in working class style?
    (ii) What did they intend to do about it?

(l) Why was the hope of another house for many working class families 'more a dream than a possibility'?

3 SOCIAL CLASS: UPBRINGING AND OPPORTUNITY
Study the three life histories below very carefully, making notes about parents, family background, income, education, life experiences, attitudes, present employment, interests, and aspirations for the future. Using your notes, write an essay to compare the ways in which their social class has affected the life, work and behaviour of each of the three people.

(a) *Christopher Gotch, Architect*
The youngest of three, I was born at Kettering, Northamptonshire, in 1923.

Until the age of five I played hide and seek, much as I have been doing since, in the ample grounds of the family house before being despatched, presumably because I had become an embarrassment to my parents, to boarding school. There I remained in seclusion until a road accident and the outbreak of the Second World War forced my father to economize.

Freed from the hell that was Marlborough College, at sixteen my father forced me into the LDV (forerunner of the Home Guard); that and the early blitz and a year at home were sufficient to induce me to falsify my age to join the RAF in 1941. After a year's training mostly in Canada, I joined a fighter squadron as a tenderfoot commissioned pilot, only to be wounded at Dieppe a few months later. In 1943 I was posted to the India and Burma theatre; a squadron leader at twenty-one, flight commander of a mosquito squadron, I was wounded again.

I qualified as an architect in 1953; my first private commission came two years before and more followed until by 1958 it was clear that I had to decide between remaining a salaried architect or developing my own business. Since 1960 I have practised alone.

During this period I became involved in the community life of Hampstead, where I have lived since 1947, believing that it provides the most nearly perfect urban environment of anywhere in Britain and one especially suitable for children in their early years. Realizing that architects cannot work in a vacuum, I have over the years been instrumental in forming the New Hampstead (Civic) Society, the Camden Society of Architects and, rather of a different nature, a professional Opera Company, Group Eight. As a consequence of these activities I am now an itinerant, persuasive lecturer on architecture, a pontificator on the environment in a local weekly paper, and have been an RIBA award and Civic Trust award juror.

Author of five books, only one of which has been published, it's clear that I am an arch-dabbler, for I also paint and sculpture in wood, and when disgusted with all these pursuits turn to rug making. These are of inordinate size and occupy me for years – a sort of permanent labour of Hercules. Opera is an obsession and keeps my wayward emotions at bay, while photography panders to my frustrated creativity.

Through studying Robert Mylne, an obscure eighteenth-century architect and engineer, on whom I have published several articles and am now considered an authority, I discovered the canals of Britain, a different section of which I explore each year by boat in an orgy of getting away from it all.

From *Work 2*, edited by Ronald Fraser

(b) *Bryan Slater, Assembly Line Worker*
I was born in 1933, in Nottingham. My father happened to be on the dole at the time, and wasn't able to get work until the war started. I didn't think it strange,

having him at home all the time, but sometimes it was unpleasant if he was feeling particularly low.

I did my bit of schooling at a secondary modern, but spent more time playing truant than in the classroom. The schoolboard man came so many times to our house that one would have thought he lodged there. I used to write a note for the teacher saying I was sick, sign it with my mother's name, and go fishing or looking for bird's eggs or take some of my brother's books and sit by the Trent, reading. I learned more by myself than I could have at school where most of the time was spent in prayers, thanking God for the slice of bread and jam we'd had for breakfast. I never knew there had been a revolution in Russia, and didn't know the meaning of the word 'revolution' until I started work and joined a union.

My father, brothers and sisters worked in the Raleigh bicycle factory, and that was where I went. I worked in the three-speed shop, and now that money started coming in I often went to the pictures, sometimes with my father. He could never see enough gangster films, and when I asked him why he told me he'd been carted off by two buck policemen for getting too much into debt. He got six months in gaol, and said he'd have got off except that he told the judge what he thought of him and the whole idea of being pulled in because he'd only tried to get some food for his kids. His favourite scene in any film was when a policeman was shot.

At eighteen I was called up. The only good thing the army taught me was how to handle a rifle and fire a machine gun, which I think might come in useful one day.

I met my wife just after coming out of the army. She was a Shropshire girl, and that's where we live now. Our council flat overlooks the village cemetery, and sometimes from my window I can see the men digging holes and later, especially at weekends, they carry the bodies in.

I am a member of the A.E.U. and the Labour party. I hope that my daughter gets a better education than I did; I don't want her starting work at fifteen. My main pastimes are cooking, fishing and reading. I have always wanted to know how to paint, to make pictures.

From *Work*, edited by Ronald Fraser

(c) *Richard Fry, Accountant*

I was born in Kilburn, London, in 1925, where I lived until I was nine. My family then moved to a housing estate in Southall where I stayed until I married.

My father was the son of a Welsh horse-and-cart greengrocer. Unwilling to return to Wales after the First World War, in which he was wounded, he went into domestic service for a year or two, where he met my mother, who was also in service. She was the daughter of a roadmender. Later my father got a job as a porter on the London Electric Railway. He was a staunch trade unionist, active in the 1926 strike; at sixty-five he retired with a pension of 13s. a week.

I left elementary school at Easter, 1939, and started accountancy a couple of years later at the age of sixteen. I qualified in 1949. Five years later, having built up a small connexion by working in the evenings, I was able to start my own practice. During that time and subsequently my illness deteriorated very considerably; today I need assistance to walk, but this has not limited my activities.

I am a director of a number of companies. I like poetry, the theatre, music, politics, good food and drink, and animals. I dislike racialists, nationalists, censorship, religions, ungenerosity. Politically I am on the left – a convinced nuclear disarmer for the U.K. and opposed to the present large defence spending. I would spend more on education, the social services, etc. But I regard the biggest (and so far untackled) need is for a crash programme to increase national income substantially, not just by 2 per cent a year.

From *Work*, edited by Ronald Fraser

4 SPEECH

(i) *The Two Forms of Language*

It has been suggested by Dr Basil Bernstein (1961) that there are, in fact, two quite different forms of language, and that many children, because they do not come into close contact with children outside their own social class, or because they are not spoken to enough, are limited in their early years to only one of these forms, to future detriment of their intellectual development.

Middle-class children, believes Dr. Bernstein, are brought up in an environment where language is often quite formal, and the speech mode is one where the structure and syntax are relatively difficult to predict.

Working-class environments are characterized by a form of speech that is very direct, unambiguous and closely identified with the speaker. 'It is a form of relatively condensed speech in which certain meanings are restricted and the possibility of their elaboration is reduced.' Where the middle-class mother might, for example, say to her child: 'I'd rather you made less noise, darling', the working-class mother might say: 'Shut up!' But it is not merely the range of words that matter here, but the way they are used. A child growing up in an environment where words are not simply a means of instantly expressed desires or imperatives, but of a wide and infinitely-complex network of expression at an early age can become mentally flexible in his approach to the world. Life becomes graded into a variety of very fine shades, differing from but allied to one another. The speaker is able to use words like mixing colours on a palette, taking great care to pick those which most closely match his precise meaning. This is not just a matter of a wide vocabulary, but of an understanding of the nuances of language.

From *The Pre-School Years*, by William van der Eyken

(a) Give two reasons to explain why many children are limited to only one type of language.

(b) What type of language is experienced by children growing up in a middle class home?

(c) What type of language is experienced by children growing up in a working class home?

(d) Give an illustration from your own knowledge to compare the *different ways* in which a middle class and working class mother might express the same idea to her children.

(e) What difference to ways of thinking and experiencing the world does the complicated language make possible?

(ii) *No Communication*

(Mr Gillow is training to be a teacher at a University Department of Education and has come himself from an upper middle class background. Keith is from a working class home and expects to be leaving school at 16. In this extract Mr Gillow describes an afternoon they spent together.)

Keith and I visited the castle in pursuance of his interest in history. On reaching the museum there he told me he had already been some time ago, but was quite willing to co-operate with my wish to make the visit. We wandered from room to room, Keith showing particular interest in agricultural implements. He has an uncle with a farm in Herts. which he has visited. We discussed the great advances in technological spheres over the last hundred years in comparison with previous historical methods of farming which had remained virtually similar for centuries. Keith was also interested in the old methods of torture and poacher-catching devices, etc.; he was able to recall some of the exhibits from his previous visit to say a little about them. We then visited the keep, which Keith knew. He was able to show me the way up to it and to demonstrate the impressive view from the top. During the afternoon we discussed a wide variety of topics, such as ancient history, education, his science lessons, parents and space travel, world poverty and politics. Most of these discussions consisted of me giving my opinions and Keith either agreeing or disagreeing, together with a short comment from him. He appeared to be interested in all this and seems to have a wide range of sympathies, but is constantly held back by his chronic inability to form articulate sentences or a succession of remarks.

From *Young Teachers and Reluctant Learners*, by Hannam, Stephenson and Smyth

(a) How would you describe Mr Gillow's form of language?

(b) Give two illustrations from the passage which give a clue to Keith's form of language.

(c) Mr Gillow talked about a vast range of subjects which he said 'appeared' to interest Keith. Make a list of these.

(d) What, in fact, did Keith show most interest in?

(e) What was Mr Gillow's opinion of Keith?

(f) Do you think that the relationship between Keith and Mr Gillow was a good one? Give your reasons.

(g) What advice would you give Mr Gillow about language in his teaching career?

(iii) *Accent*

(Miss Upton has just learned that Hugh's sister is at university while he plans to leave school as soon as he can.)

Miss Upton: You didn't tell me that before.

Hugh: Well no need to.

Miss Upton: Oh, interesting though.

Hugh: She was headgirl of the Vale school.

Miss Upton: Was she?

Hugh: Yeah.

Laurie: Headgirl?

Miss Upton: Where's the Vale?

Laurie: It's the highest school in the city for girls. You know, poncy school isn't it? Only your sister wasn't poncy.

Hugh: She is.

Miss Upton: Oh, she is is she?

Hugh: Yeah . . . she speaks all wrong.

Miss Upton: How does she speak then?

Hugh: All poncy!

Miss Upton: How does someone speak poncy? Do I speak poncy?

Hugh: No (laughter)

Miss Upton: Oh, saved from that then! Give me an imitation of somebody speaking poncy.

Laurie: Oh . . . (laughter) . . . he don't know hisself.

Hugh (exaggeratedly)*:* 'Oh dash it old boy' and all that.

Miss Upton: Have you ever heard anyone speak like that?

Hugh: No.

Miss Upton: I don't know, some people speak like that naturally because that's the way their families always spoke.

Hugh: Yeah and all those lords and all that.

Miss Upton: Well, I don't know about them. There are people I know who speak like that at university and it's quite natural to them, you don't mind it, it doesn't grate on your nerves.

From *Young Teachers and Reluctant Learners* by Hannam, Stephenson and Smyth

(a) Explain *in your own words* the boys' opinion of the Vale School.

(b) Why do you think they hold this opinion?

(c) What is Hugh's opinion of his sister's accent?

(d) Miss Upton tries to show why some people speak differently from others. Explain *in your own words* what she means.

(e) In what way can the term 'social mobility' be applied to Hugh's sister?

5 DRESS AND APPEARANCE

Look at the picture very carefully.

(a) What sort of shop is this?

(b) What do the goods on the pavement tell you about the area in which the photograph was taken?

(c) Look at the women's clothes. Where might they have been bought? What sort of quality are they?

(d) Look at their hands and faces. What do you notice about them?

(e) Which social class do these women belong to? Give your reasons in full.

6 BEHAVIOUR AND ATTITUDES

(i) *Family Care*

Study the table of statistics very carefully, then answer the questions below:

(a) Which class of mothers seems to be the most efficient with regard to bringing up their children?

	Middle Class Mothers		Working Class Mothers	
	Upper	Lower	Upper	Lower
	%	%	%	%
Highest standards of infant care	53.1	37.0	22.1	15.1
Highest standards of infant management	66.2	49.4	34.5	28.1
Good use of medical services	78.9	67.4	54.2	42.4
High interest in school progress	41.7	21.7	11.4	5.0
Desires grammar school place	73.3	73.3	57.7	48.8
Late school leaving wished	77.6	40.7	21.7	12.9
Shows at least 4 of the above	81.0	58.0	34.6	19.6

From *The Home and the School*, by J. W. B. Douglas

(b) Which class of mothers seems to be the least informed about the benefits of the welfare state for their children?

(c) Which mothers put most pressure on their children to perform well at school?

(d) Which class of mothers shows the most inconsistency in attitude to their child's schooling?

(e) Write in your own words a clear explanation of the statistical material presented in the table.

(ii) *Adolescent Boys*

The Working-Class Boy He went to a secondary modern or possibly 'comprehensive' school and left at 15. He did not like school; on the whole he was not critical of the teachers and he approved of most of the rules, though he thought the lessons of little value and school generally rather remote from life. He is most likely to have a skilled or semi-skilled manual job which he is broadly content with. When he is asked what job he would like to do in ten years' time if he could choose, he will probably say the job he has now, which is also the one he 'expects' to have in the future: 'Plumber's mate now, expect to be a plumber, and if I could choose, that's what I'd like to be'. He expects to marry, probably before he is 25. He is more likely to spend money than to save it, and to say that one should 'enjoy oneself' rather than 'work hard'.

The Lower Working-Class Boy He went to a secondary modern school and, like the 'working-class' boy, left at 15. But he did not like school: he disliked the

41

teachers and the school regime, as well as thinking the lessons 'useless'. His job is manual, and is more likely to be unskilled or semi-skilled than skilled. He is discontented with his work and particularly the lack of prospects. He has probably had at least three jobs since leaving school, sometimes many more. He does not get on too well with his parents and he dislikes the police. He is more likely than other boys to say that he does not intend to marry at all or that he does not know whether he will. He rejects, even more firmly than his 'working-class' fellows, the idea of 'deferred gratification'. It is probably from boys like this that the seriously delinquent are drawn.

The Middle-Class Boy He went to a grammar or 'comprehensive' school and left at 16 or over. He liked school and approved of the teachers and the school rules; unlike his 'working-class' counterpart, he regarded the school curriculum as 'useful'. If he is not still at school – he may be until 18 – his present job is as a clerk, a salesman or a junior executive. His father is often a shopkeeper or clerk. The boy likes his work, and is looking forward to moving up the career ladder as he gets older. He believes in saving money, and in studying and working hard so as to 'get on'. He expects to marry, but this is more likely to be after 25 than before. His work and interests are outside Bethnal Green; he does not particularly like the district and looks to the day when he will live somewhere 'better'.

From *Adolescent Boys of East London,* by Willmott and Young

(a) Which of the three boys was:
    (i) most antagonistic to school?
    (ii) most complacent about school?
    (iii) most in favour of school?
(b) Which of the boys stayed longest at school?
(c) Which of the boys was likely to:
    (i) work hardest at school?
    (ii) work intermittently at school?
    (iii) do as little school work as possible?
(d) In the world of employment which boy was:
    (i) the most restless at work?
    (ii) the most ambitious at work?
    (iii) the most satisfied with his job?
(e) What are the future prospects for each of the three boys in terms of:
    (i) family?
    (ii) standard of living?

(iii) *'It Isn't Cricket'*
(A working class boy who attends a middle class grammar school meets a new set of behaviour expectations on the games field)

'Simon Carpenter was Captain, and he was dead keen that we all walk on the field in a straight line behind him, like professionals. Well, I'd never do that, nor would my pal Hopkins. And then the master, Rylands, he always insisted that we had whites, white shirt, white shorts, white shoes, white socks, all dressed *properly*. Well, George Hopkins would come along wearing green corduroy pants and one of those tee-shirts with cowboys across the front, and I'd wear my shirt outside my trousers. No . . . I don't seem to have that certain something that makes cricketers and prefects and officers. I don't know what it is.'

From *Education and the Working-Class*, by Jackson and Marsden

(a) What recognition of leadership by his team did the school cricket captain expect?

(b) How would boys at your school walk on to the sports field?

(c) (i) What type of behaviour did the schoolmaster insist upon?

   (ii) What do you think were his reasons for this?

(d) How did the boy and his friend George show their refusal to conform?

(e) The boy says, 'I don't seem to have that certain something that makes cricketers and prefects and officers'. What exactly does he mean by this remark?

(iv) *'Putting on a show'*

'Now take this here Prince Charles. I think it's a real tragedy that lad hasn't been sent to a proper school. Just an ordinary school in a decent area, a local day school. If he mixed with the ordinary lads, he'd know summat, and they'd know summat. I don't know what they're frightened of. Are they frightened of the Royal Family knowing how we live? I remember Princess Elizabeth as she was then coming to Huddersfield. The way they decorated it up! The way they dolled the mills up! And the way we had to go to work in special overalls that day! We weren't allowed to dirty them, we daren't do a spot of work in case we got a bit of dirt on us (mine's a filthy job, and you can't work two minutes without being black all over). But no, you'd got to be bright and clean for when she saw us. Now that's all wrong. Wrong altogether! I've tried to fathom this out but I can't study it out no way. Don't they like the way Huddersfield looks? Do they think she won't like it if she sees it? Nay, it's altogether wrong.'

From *Education and the Working-Class*, by Jackson and Marsden

(a) (i) Which social class does the speaker belong to?

   (ii) Give three illustrations from the passage to support your answer.

(b) (i) If not 'a proper school', what sort of school did Prince Charles attend?

   (ii) Why does the speaker consider this a mistake?

(c) (i) In what ways did Huddersfield 'put on a show' for the Queen?

(ii) What were the reasons for this?

(d) Do you agree with the fact that:

(i) Prince Charles should not attend an ordinary school?

(ii) towns and industries should be 'decorated' for a visit by the Royal Family?

Give well considered reasons to support your opinions.

Chapter 3

Culture

Culture and Sub-Culture

When the word 'culture' is used by sociologists it has a special meaning. All of us have heard the word used to describe ballet or opera, the theatre, painting, classical music and literature – all that is thought to be the best in the creative arts. For sociologists, however, the word culture refers to the total way of life of a society. It is made up of its members' customs, traditions and beliefs; their behaviour, dress and language; their work; their living arrangements; their relationships with each other; and their attitudes to life. Everything in fact which they hold in common with other members of the same society. When we talk about American culture, or African culture, or Turkish culture, we mean the total way of life of the people of America, Africa or Turkey.

Each society has its own particular culture, which has developed throughout its history and which is passed on from one generation to the next. New members born into society do not inherit their culture biologically – it has to be learned. All people born in Britain, therefore, will learn the British way of life and will grow up to have certain beliefs, attitudes and patterns of behaviour in common which will distinguish them from, for example, people growing up in China, Morocco, or Brazil.

As we have already seen, societies are made up of various groups of people who have their own distinctive behaviour. This typical group behaviour is also a kind of culture, but because groups exist within and as a smaller part of the total society the term sub-culture is used.

For instance, we can talk about the working class sub-culture to refer to the particular way of life of working class people which differentiates them from the middle and upper classes. We can also talk about the teenage sub-culture to refer to the typical dress, behaviour, attitudes, and tastes of young people, which differentiate them from their parents or their grandparents. Gypsies, criminals, Catholic nuns and many other identifiable groups all possess specific sub-cultures within the total culture of Britain.

The main thing which makes people different in various parts of the world is largely their possession of differing cultures. If you had been transported at birth to a peasant's cottage in Italy, or brought up in a nomad's family in central Africa, your culture would be that of your adopted family and in no way that of a British teenager.

The best way to illustrate this is to look at two examples of other people's culture, that of the Bushmen and the Bedouin. Read and discuss them together, then attempt the written work.

The Bushmen of the Kalihari

Two hundred years ago great numbers of Bushmen lived a stone-age existence in much of southern Africa, but the arrival of the Europeans and the Bantu in the early nineteenth century began a progressive massacre of their tribes and a destruction of their way of life. Today small numbers of Bushmen can still be found in the Kalihari desert, where they continue their traditional way of life untouched by progress.

PHYSICAL CHARACTERISTICS

The bushman was not a dwarf or pigmy, but a little man about five feet in height. He was well and sturdily made. His shoulders were broad, but his hands and feet were extraordinarily small and finely modelled. His ankles were slim, his leg muscles supple, and he could run like the wind, fast and for great distances. When on the move he hardly ever walked but, like the springbuck or wild dog, travelled at an easy trot. His skin was loose and as he grew up became very creased and incredibly wrinkled. When he laughed, which he did easily, his face broke into innumerable little folds and pleats of a most subtle and endearing criss-cross pattern.

His life as a hunter made it of vital importance that he should be able to store great reserves of food in his body. As a result, his stomach, after he had eaten to capacity, made even a man look like a pregnant woman. In a good hunting season, his figure was like that of a Rubens' cupid, protruding in front and even more behind. Yes, that was another of the unique characteristics of this little Bushman. He had a behind which served him rather as the hump serves the camel! In this way nature enabled him to store a reservoir of valuable fats and carbo-hydrates against drought and hunger. His colour was a lovely apricot yellow. Although he wore no clothes, his skin never burnt dark in the sun. His eyes were of a deep brown, penetrating and accurate, and he could see things far away when other people could discern nothing.

NXOU AT HOME

We were among the first four shelters before we had even seen them, so discreetly were they made and so naturally did they blend with the growth and colour around them. Basically they were of bee-hive design, solidly built and carefully roofed with branches of fern and tufts of grass. Each had a tree at the back to support it and from some of the branches hung strips of venison drying out in

46

the wind and shade. The floors of the shelters were scooped out in places to make them more comfortable for the hips of the people sleeping in them, and the interiors were almost bare of decoration or utensils. But where the women slept hung strings of the white beads and ivory headbands made out of shells of ostrich eggs, and along the sides of the shelters were rows of ostrich egg-shells securely placed upright in the sand, plugged with grass and presumably filled with water.

Outside the first shelter, a middle-aged woman sat diligently pounding the seeds of the tsamma, the Kalahari melon which sustains man and beast with food and moisture in the long, hot months between the rains. The stamping block is the Bushman woman's most precious possession: a large pestle and mortar carved out of iron-wood. Wherever she goes she carries it with her to make meal out of nuts and seeds of melons and grass, and to pulverise dried meat for toothless children and old people.

In front of the second shelter sat Nxou's father stringing a bow. His wife at his side was cooking something in a small clay pot on a tiny fire which hardly made any smoke. At the third shelter another middle-aged man was repairing one of the long rods used to fish in holes in the ground for spring-hares, porcupines, badgers, ground squirrels, and other animals that live underneath the Kalihari sand. Outside the last of the shelters sat two of the oldest people I have ever seen. They were Nxou's grandparents and the skins of both were so creased and stained with life, weather, and time that they might have been dark brown parchment covered with some Oriental script. Both had serene expressions on their faces and they looked continually from one to the other as if in constant need of reassurance that the miracle of being together after so many years was indeed still real.

The old lady I could see was already beginning to feel the heat. From time to time she put her hand deep into a hole beside her to pull out a handful of cool sand which she scattered over her naked body for relief. I have often seen elephants do the same thing with their trunks. She did this as daintily as some Mongol lady fanning herself, and was as shy as a young girl, immediately looking away from us when she caught our eye, and then glancing coyly back out of the corner of her slanted eyes when her curiosity became too great.

When I asked if that was the whole community Nxou shook his head. The young women and children, he said, were already out in the desert seeking for food. The other half of his people were grouped around five similar shelters about a mile away.

These shelters were almost exact copies of the first with people doing the same sorts of things, except that one man was busy re-dipping his arrows in newly prepared poison, and another softening a duiker skin with incredible swiftness by squeezing the juice of a large bulb on to it and wringing the moist skin between his hands. While we were there the younger women began coming home. They were all naked except for a leather wrap hung by a strap from one shoulder and tied round their waists. The hem of the wrap was decorated with ostrich-shell beads and around the smooth yellow necks of the younger women hung rows of necklaces made of the same beads. In that sun, against those apricot skins, the necklaces shone like jewels. Each woman carried a shawl of skin tied into a bundle which she placed on the sand and undid, taking out the amazing variety of roots and tubers they had collected in the desert, as well as dozens of ostrich egg-shells filled with water.

While the hunters were out the older people did the maintenance work of the community: repaired the bows and arrows and the long 'fishing rods', and prepared the poison used in hunting. This they did out of a deadly compound of a mysterious grub found in summer at the end-root of a certain desert bush, powdered cobra poison, and a gum produced by chewing a special aloe blade in the mouth and then mixing the extract in a wooden cup with the other powders. They also cured and tanned the skins of the buck brought home by the hunters.

They were natural botanists and chemists and had an unbelievable knowledge of the properties of desert plants. A bulb gave them the acid to remove the hair from the skin without damage, another softened it in a remarkably short time.

The older women, in their spare moments, made beads out of broken ostrich egg-shells and strung them into necklaces or the broad shining bands which they wore around their heads for ceremonial occasions. Hour after hour they would sit chipping humbly and delicately with the sharp end of a springbuck ram's bone at a fragment of shell in order to produce one little round white disc from the brittle and fragile raw material.

Every woman and girl child possessed several necklaces and at least one glittering headband, apart from the beads used to decorate the leather wrap, shawl, and shoulder satchel which were their only covering. Sometimes, too, they carved greater beads out of a crimson root and amber wood, and this combination of ivory white shell, crimson, and amber jewellery on the smooth apricot skins between the firm round breasts of the younger women seemed to me as truly belonging as a ruby garland against the skin of a Hindu deity.

HUNTING

The bushman before all else was a hunter. He kept no cattle, sheep or goats except in rare instances where he had been in prolonged contact with foreigners. He did not cultivate the land and therefore grew no food. Although everywhere his women and children dug the earth with their deft grubbing sticks for edible bulbs and roots and, in season, harvested veld and bush for berries and fruit, their happiness depended mainly on the meat which he provided. He hunted in the first place with bow and arrow and spear. The heads of his arrows were dipped in a poison compounded from the grubs, roots, and glands of the reptiles of the land and he himself had such a respect for the properties of his own poison that he never went anywhere without the appropriate antidote in a little skin wallet tied securely to his person.

He was so natural a botanist and so expert an organic chemist that he used different poisons on different animals, the strongest for the eland and the lion and less powerful variants for the smaller game. His arrows were made of flint or bone until he came to barter for iron with those about to become his enemies. As an archer he was without equal and could hit a moving buck at 150 yards.

But he not only hunted with bow and arrow. In the rivers and streams he constructed traps beautifully woven out of reeds and buttressed with young karee wood or harde-kool, and so caught basketfuls of lovely golden bream, or fat olive-green barbel. Hard-by among the singing reeds he dug pits with a cunningly-covered spike in the centre in order to trap the nocturnal hippopotamus whose sweet lard meant more to him than foie-gras to any gourmet.

On top of his great daring and resource as a hunter, he was also subtle. He never seems to have attempted to accomplish by force what could be achieved by wit. The Bushman would, for example, use the lion as a hunting dog. When his normal methods of hunting failed him he would frighten the game in the direction of a hungry lion. He would let the lion kill and eat enough only to still its hunger, but not enough to make it lazy. Then the Bushman would drive the lion off with smoke and fire, and move in to eat the rest of the kill. In this way he would follow a favourite lion about from kill to kill and it was extraordinary how he and the lion came to respect their strange partnership.

Yet with all this hunting, snaring, and trapping, the Bushman's relationship with the animals and birds of Africa was never merely one of hunter and hunted; his knowledge of the plants, trees, and insects of the land never just the knowledge of a consumer of food. On the contrary, he knew the animal and vegetable life, the rocks, and the stones of Africa as they had never been known since. The proof of all this is there in his paintings on his beloved rock for those who can see with their hearts as well as their eyes. There the animals of Africa still live as he knew them and as no European or Bantu artist has yet been able to portray them.

TWO BUSHMEN DRAWING WATER FROM THE DESERT

The water supply which never failed the bushmen was hidden, safe from evaporation of sun and wind, deep beneath the sand. Near the deepest excavation Bauxhau knelt down and dug into the same to arm's length. Towards the end some moist sand but not water appeared. Then he took a tube almost five feet long made out of the stem of a bush with a soft core, wound about four inches of dry grass lightly around one end presumably to act as a kind of filter against the fine drift sand, inserted it into the hole and packed the sand back into it, stamping it down with his feet. He then took some empty ostrich egg-shells from Xhooxham and wedged them upright into the sand beside the tube, produced a little stick one end of which he inserted into the opening in the shell and the other into the corner of his mouth. Then he put his lips to the tube. For about two minutes he sucked mightily without any result. His broad shoulders heaved with the immense effort and sweat began to run like water down his back. But at last the miracle happened and so suddenly that I had an impulse loudly to cheer. A bubble of pure bright water came out of the corner of Bauxhau's mouth, clung to the little stick, and ran straight down its side into the shell without spilling one precious drop!

From *The Lost World of the Kalihari* and *The Heart of the Hunter*, by Laurens Van der Post

The Bedu of Arabia

The Bedu are the nomadic camel-breeding tribes of the Arabian desert, usually known in English as Bedouin. The following extracts are by Wilfred Thesiger, who spent several years in their company.

CHARACTERISTICS

Their nomad life allowed the Bedu few possessions; everything not a necessity was an encumbrance. The clothes in which they stood, their weapons and saddlery, a few pots and waterskins and goat-hair shelters, were all they owned; those and the animals whose welfare regulated their every move and for whose sake they cheerfully suffered every hardship. Arrogant, individualistic and intensely proud, they never willingly accepted any man as their master and would rather die than be shamed. The most democratic of people, they yet valued lineage highly, and for centuries had guarded the purity of their blood with the dagger. To their sheikhs they accorded a measure of respect due to their descent, but gave them no more unless they earned it. The head of a tribe was the first among equals. He had no servants and paid retainers to enforce his will, or to effect his judgements. His tribesmen followed him only so long as he commanded their respect, and he ruled them only so long as they obeyed him; if he displeased them they followed another of his family, and his guest tent was left empty. Living crowded together in the open desert, no concealment was possible, every act was noted and every word was overheard. Inveterate gossips, they knew all that passed, and the question, 'What is news?' succeeded every greeting. If a man distinguished himself, his fellows paraded him through the encampment on a camel shouting, 'God whiten the face of so-and-so!' If he had disgraced himself, they drove him forth with cries of 'God blacken the face of so-and-so!', and he became an outcast. Avid for acclaim, they went to great lengths to win it, and many of their acts were theatrical in consequence. Though jealous of others, they were staunchly loyal to their fellow tribesmen; to betray a companion was the blackest sin, far worse than murder to people whose disregard for human life enabled them in settlement of a blood feud to knife an unarmed herdsboy with a jest. But while they were callous about their own sufferings, and the sufferings of others, they were never deliberately cruel. Their honour was easily touched and they were quick to repay an insult, real or imagined, but usually they were humorous and light-hearted.

Theirs was a character of opposites. Garrulous by nature, they were always careful of their dignity, and would sit in silence for hours on formal occasions. Indifferent to natural beauty, they had a passionate love for poetry. Often impractically generous, they would give away their only shirt to someone who asked for it. Their hospitality was legendary – a man would think nothing of killing one of his precious camels to feed a stranger who had chanced on his tent; but at heart they were avaricious, with all the Semite's love of money. They were deeply religious and saw the hands of God in everything. It would have been as inconceivable for them to doubt his existence as to blaspheme. Yet they were not naturally fanatical, nor were they passively fatalistic. In their hard lives they fought to the bitter end, and then accepted their fate with dignity, as the will of God.

TRIBAL LAW

The society in which the Bedu live is tribal. Everyone belongs to a tribe and all members of the same tribe are in some degree kinsmen, since they are descended from a common ancestor. The closer the relationship the stronger is the loyalty which a man feels for his fellow tribesmen, and this loyalty overrides personal feelings, except in extreme cases. In time of need a man instinctively supports his fellow tribesmen, just as they in like case support him. There is no security in the desert for an individual outside the framework of his tribe. This makes it possible for tribal law, which is based on consent, to work among the most individualistic race in the world, since in the last resort a man who refuses to accept a tribal decision can be ostracized. It is therefore a strange fact that tribal law can only work in conditions of anarchy and breaks down as soon as peace is imposed upon the desert, since under peaceful conditions a man who resents a judgement can refuse to be bound by it, and if necessary can leave his tribe and live by himself. There is no central authority inside the tribe which can enforce the judgement.

PRAYER

I would watch old Tamtaim washing before he prayed. Every act had to be performed exactly and in order. He washed his face, hands and feet, sucked water into his nostrils, put wet fingers into his ears, and passed wet hands over the top of his head. Tamtaim then swept the ground before him, placed his rifle in front of him and then prayed facing toward Mecca. He stood upright, bent forward, his hands on his knees, knelt and then bowed down till his forehead touched the ground. Several times he performed these ritual movements, slowly and impressively, while he recited the formal prayer. Sometimes, after he had finished his prayers, he intoned long passages from the Koran, and the very sound of the words had the quality of great poetry. Muslims pray at dawn, at noon, in the afternoon, at sunset and after dark.

CONFIRMING IDENTITY

Bedu can tell as much about camels from their tracks as they can about tribesmen from their dress and appearance. Every man knew the individual tracks of his own camels, and some of them could remember the tracks of nearly every camel they had seen. They could tell at a glance from the depth of the footprints whether a camel was ridden or free, and whether it was in calf. By studying strange tracks they could tell the area from which the camel came. Camels from the Sands, for instance, have soft soles to their feet, marked with tattered strips of loose skin, whereas if they come from the gravel plains their feet are polished smooth. Bedu could tell the tribe to which a camel belonged, for the different tribes have different breeds of camel, all of which can be distinguished by their tracks. From looking at their droppings they could often deduce where a camel had been grazing, and they could certainly tell when it had last been watered, and from their knowledge of the country they could probably tell where. Bedu are always well informed about the politics of the desert. They know the alliances and enmities of the tribes and can guess which tribes would raid each other. No Bedu will ever miss a chance of exchanging news with anyone he meets, and he will ride far out of his way to get fresh news.

Meeting a stranger, they can tell which tribe he belongs to by numerous signs perceptible at once to their discerning eyes: whether he wears his cartridge-belt buckled tightly or sagging low in front, whether he wears his head cloth loosely or more closely wound round his head; the stitching on his shirt, the folds of his loin cloths, the leather cover in which he carries his rifle, the pattern on his saddle bags, the way he has folded his rug above them, even the way he walks, all these reveal his identity. But above all they can tell from a man's speech to which tribe he belongs.

MEALTIMES

The Bedu squat round the dish of rice over which gravy has been poured, each with his portion of meat in front of him, and dipping his right hand into the rice. They mould the handful which they have taken in the palm of the hand until it becomes a ball, and then put it neatly into their mouths with fingers and thumb. An Arab always feeds with his right hand and avoids if possible touching food with his left hand, for this is the unclean hand with which he washes after he has relieved himself. It is even bad manners to pass anyone anything with this hand or to accept anything with it.

There is always trouble if meat is not divided by lot. Someone immediately says that he has been given more than his share, and tries to hand a piece to someone else. Then there is much arguing and swearing by God, with everyone insisting that he has been given too much, and finally a deadlock ensues which can only be settled by casting lots for the meat – as should have been done in the first place. An Arab never grumbles that he has received less than his share. Such behaviour would be inconceivable to the Bedu, for they are careful never to appear greedy, and quick to notice anyone who is.

Arabs never distinguish between what is eatable and what is not, but always between food which is lawful and food which is forbidden. No Muslim may eat pork, blood or the flesh of an animal which has not had its throat cut while it was still alive. Most of them will not eat meat slaughtered by anyone other than a Muslim, or by a boy who is still uncircumcised.

From *Arabian Sands* and *The Marsh Arabs*, by Wilfred Thesiger

You and Your Culture

Imagine a man from Mars sitting with notebook and pencil in hand in the observation room of his U.F.O. just above this classroom. What notes about British culture would he make?

Firstly, that young people in this society go to schools or specialised institutions to learn information and appropriate behaviour. For this occasion they wear a special type of uniform – clothing which they don't wear at other times if they can help it, but with the boys' dress easily distinguishable from the girls'.

Secondly, he would see an older person in the room standing near a blackboard and talking to the children. Even though they outnumber the adult, they are under his influence, and are doing what he says. Obviously in this culture our man from Mars would deduce a respect by the young for those in authority over them.

Thirdly, he would notice that as the teacher talks to the children they put up their hands to answer questions and give their information when asked. No one is shouting another down, climbing up the wall, leaping out of the window, or eating fish and chips. The teacher isn't smoking or drinking a pint of beer. Obviously there are some unwritten rules of behaviour in the classroom that everyone adheres to.

Fourthly, looking about the walls of the room, he may see books, charts and pictures, a film screen and projector, perhaps a television set. All this would help him to describe this as a literate culture with developed media of mass communication.

Finally, the building itself and its furniture, obviously made by machinery and complicated industrial processes, would show this as an advanced society which had set up factories and methods of mass production.

When the bell goes, the children get up to leave and are replaced by another group looking exactly the same and behaving in a similar way.

Up and down the country in all kinds of schools you will find a part of our culture which can be easily identified. There is nothing inherent in us which says we should behave in such a way; we have learned this as part of our culture just as we learn the many other aspects of our way of life.

We shall go on to study further cultural aspects in later chapters of this book. Others you will also meet next year in Book 2. Always remember that while the behaviour of other societies may seem strange and even amusing, it is as natural and acceptable to them as your classroom behaviour is to you.

Discussion and Written Work

1 On an outline map of Africa mark in the areas where the Bushmen and the Bedouin can be found.

2 (a) What special physical characteristics are peculiar to the Bushmen?
(b) Describe as accurately as you can a Bushman's home. (Illustrate with a sketch.)
(c) What does the Bushman use ostrich egg-shells for?
(d) What is the main diet of the Bushmen?
(e) How are Bushmen women dressed?
(f) What work is done in a Bushmen community by:
    (i) the men?
    (ii) the women?
    (iii) the children?
    (iv) the elderly?
(g) What special skills are characteristic of Bushmen hunters?
(h) Explain as carefully as you can how the Bushmen obtained water from the desert.
(i) What proof remains to record the characteristics of the dying race of Bushmen?

3 (a) What are the typical characteristics of a nomadic way of life?
(b) Describe fully the personality characteristics typical of the Bedu, and for each suggest which aspects of their way of life could account for these.
(c) How is Bedu society divided up?
(d) Explain the point of contact which keeps the tribes together.
(e) What religion are the Bedu?
(f) What clues help the Bedu to deduce:
    (i) the identity of camels?
    (ii) the identity of strangers?

Why is this still a vital skill in Arabian society?

(g) Why does an Arab never eat with his left hand?

(h) What other special rituals surround Bedouin eating habits?

4 Wilfred Thesiger also says of the Bedu, 'I listened to old men who spoke of events which had occurred a thousand years ago as if they had happened in their own youth'. Say, with your reasons, what this tells you about the culture of Bedu society.

5 What aspects of British culture would the man from Mars discover looking down on:

(a) your family group at meal times?

(b) a seaside holiday camp in August?

(c) the visit of the Royal Family to a local event?

Chapter 4

Social Research

Objectivity

Sociology, together with subjects like economics, politics and psychology, is called a social science. Because it studies people and their way of life it is often confused with journalism and literature, but this is quite wrong. Journalists and writers often observe the same things as sociologists, but when their emotions and their personal feelings are working very hard their view is always biased.

Sociologists try to prevent their personal opinions biasing what they see. They describe situations as they are, not as they imagine them or as they would like them to be, and they are always eager to test and offer scientific proof to support their findings.

As you study the sociological information in this book and carry out investigations of your own, you must try to be as objective or unbiased as you can. As soon as you allow your own particular prejudices to colour your vision, you will be accused of making value judgments which are not objective and which cannot be scientifically tested.

How the Sociologist finds out about Society

Journalists get a great deal of their news by wandering around waiting for something to happen or by stumbling across a good story almost by accident. Sociologists, however, spend a good deal of time deciding what they are going to investigate and the way they intend to do it long before any actual research is done. They start by identifying an aspect of behaviour which interests them, e.g.:

(i) Women usually seem to put their husbands and families before their own career ambitions.

(ii) Most juvenile delinquents seem to be boys from working class homes.

(iii) Conservative MPs are more likely to represent rural areas in the south of England than industrial towns in the north or mining communities in Wales.

They then want to know the reasons for this behaviour and begin to consider possible explanations. For example, it may be that women put their families before their careers because:

(a) it is part of human nature for women to bring up children and look after their husbands' homes.

(b) women are not by nature very ambitious.

(c) women's careers are not as important as men's.

(d) women have been brought up to react in this way.

Each of these possible explanations is called a hypothesis. The next step is to test which of these hypotheses (possible explanations) is correct by conducting an investigation.

Physical scientists work in laboratories with various materials and conduct complicated experiments to prove their theories or to discover new information. The social scientist must also conduct experiments, but his material is people. Because it is not possible to do the same kind of tests on people as materials, the sociologist has to use other methods of experiment and investigation. Here are three of the most important ones:

OBSERVATION

One of the best ways of studying a group of people is to spend a great deal of time observing them at close quarters. Sociologists who are principally interested in studying the day to day existence of primitive societies are called anthropologists and their methods are to go and live with the tribe they are observing for a period of time, noting, tape-recording, photographing and sharing in their daily lives.

Some sociologists who have wanted to study the behaviour of teenage gangs have become a gang member for several months, sharing in their lives and adventures. Others interested in criminals or mental patients have lived in prisons or mental hospitals with the inmates and observed and interpreted their social behaviour.

INTERVIEWS

Much valuable research has been done by interviewing individuals or groups of people. Interviews can be very short and formal during which time the interviewer asks very specific questions and notes down the respondents' replies, or they can be long and informal, sometimes lasting for several two to three hour sessions. On these occasions the sociologist usually allows the person being interviewed to talk at length and makes tape recordings of his conversation. Oscar Lewis used this method to build up character studies of poor people like Marta and Manuel in Mexico (see p. 24–27).

QUESTIONNAIRES

Questionnaires are probably the most widely used means of social research. They are quicker and cheaper than interviews and are not as likely to be biased by the personality of the people asking the questions. Sometimes they are posted, inviting people to return the completed forms; more often they are filled in by door-to-door researchers, or left and collected later.

Questionnaires must be very carefully worded if they are to be of any use, and this is a skill which you should learn to help your own investigations. The following hints will give you some idea of what to do.

Sampling

If a sociologist wanted to investigate the attitudes of soccer vandals as they kicked each other on the terraces, it would not only be very dangerous but also quite impossible to interview them all. Similarly, if he was interested in the proportion of young people who had taken drugs, he would never be able to contact every adolescent in Britain. For this reason the sociologist tries to identify a cross-section of the group he is interested in, which is totally representative of the group as a whole. This is called a sample.

SAMPLING FRAME

Suppose you intended studying the leisure-time activities of children in your school. You would not be able to question them all so you would have to draw up a sample. First you would need to get hold of a list of the names of every pupil in the school: this is called the sampling frame or the total number of possible units in the whole group.

SELECTION OF SAMPLE

There are two main ways of selecting a sample: by judgment and by probability. Judgment sampling is done by taking a sample which you judge to be representative. For example '3c is a representative class in this school'. Probability sampling is much more accurate and can be backed up by mathematical theory. There are three main kinds of probability samples.

(a) *Random Sample*

This is drawn up by picking names out of a hat.

(b) *Stratified Sample*

This is drawn up by ensuring that the proportions of the group under study are correct. For example, say for every girl in your school there are two boys, then a sample of the school must also represent the boys in the ratio 2:1.

58

(c) *Systematic Sample*

This is drawn up by taking names from the sampling frame systematically, say every tenth name on the list.

Making a Questionnaire

Designing your own questionnaire will be one of the most difficult tasks you are ever asked to do in sociology. It is very easy to write down a list of questions, but if the answers to these are going to provide the sort of information you want in a way which can be supported by statistical evidence, then your questions must be carefully worded and arranged.

Types of Questions

1 FACTUAL QUESTIONS

These are questions seeking direct information. For example:

How many brothers have you?

Where do you work?

What age did you leave school?

How long have you lived in this area?

2 MOTIVATIONAL QUESTIONS

These questions usually follow a factual question and try to discover the motives behind people's action. For example:

Why did you vote Labour last year?

Why did you leave school at fifteen?

3 CLASSIFICATION QUESTIONS

Whatever topic is being studied it is important for sociologists to know what sex, age group and social class the informant belongs to. Questions about social class or age may seem impertinent to the informant so you should explain that while the questionnaire is strictly anonymous (no names are asked for), people's opinions vary according to their age, sex and occupation and that it is the reason for including such information.

4 KNOWLEDGE QUESTIONS

It is no good asking a pupil if he would support the Schools Action Union if he does not know what it is. In such cases a knowledge question must be asked first. For example:

(a) What is the Schools Action Union?

(b) Would you personally support such a movement in your school?

Yes

No

Possibly

Don't know

5 OPINION QUESTIONS

Opinion questions can be asked in one of two ways: either by offering a series of answers and inviting the informant to tick the one most resembling his own opinion, or by leaving a space large enough for the informant to write his opinion in a few sentences of his own words.

The Wording of Questionnaires

Questionnaires should be short and straightforward with clear instructions to guide the informant. Language should be simple and questions worded in such a way that they cannot be open to several interpretations. For example, the answer to the question, 'Do you read a lot of books?' would depend very much on the type of person being questioned. 'A lot of books' to one individual might mean three books a year, in which case he would answer 'Yes'. Another person answering 'Yes' might read three books every week. In order to get round this sort of problem, it is a good idea to offer the informant a number of possible answers, asking him to tick the one which is most appropriate, e.g.:

How many books do you read on average every month?
(a) None
(b) 1–2
(c) 2–5
(d) 5–7
(e) More than 7

Similarly words can often be misleading. If you asked the question 'Which T.V. programme do you find most distasteful?' the word 'distasteful' could mean many different things to different people.

SEQUENCE

The order in which you ask the questions is important. The informant should be able to see the reasons for the order of questions and you should avoid jumping from one subject to another and then back again. For example, if you are questioning young people about the permissive society, keep all the questions referring to teenage culture together, all those about anti-social behaviour together, all those about the influence of the mass media together, and so on.

PRECISION

Questions that are asked in a vague way will only provide general answers and therefore will be difficult to turn into any kind of precise interpretation. Rather than saying 'Is T.V. harmful?' try to relate the question to people's personal experience and say 'Do you allow your own children to see T.V. programmes showing sex and violence?'

The vague question, 'How often do you play football?' could well receive the answer, 'Not very often'. Much better phrase the question like this:

'How many times a week do you play football?'
(a) never
(b) once
(c) between 2 and 4 times
(d) more than 4 times

CODED CHOICE

When you offer a series of alternative answers, one of which has to be ticked or underlined, this is called a coded choice. Because ticks are easy to count up and percentage, the interpretation of this type of material is relatively simple. You must be careful when offering a coded choice, however, that you cover all possible answers including one that allows the informant to say he doesn't know or to specify why the alternatives offered do not apply to him. For example:

What are your main reasons for going to see a particular film?
(a) Because you like the cinema?
(b) Because it's Saturday night and there's nowhere else to go?
(c) Because you have seen an advert for the film?
(d) Because a friend has recommended the film to you?
(e) Because you have read a review about the film in your newspaper?
(f) Because you like the filmstars taking part?
(g) For no particular reason?
(h) For other reasons? (please specify)

Pilot Study

When you have drawn up the questions and put them into a logical order, try them out on a few people first. This trial is called a pilot study and should reveal any weaknesses or misleading words in the questionnaire. In this way you can quickly put the problems right before contacting your proper sample.

Meeting the Public

The success of your investigation will depend upon people being prepared to answer your questions and this in turn will depend on you. Strangers will judge you by first appearances so be sure to look smart and greet them in a friendly way.

Be tactful. Don't say 'I want you to fill in this questionnaire' but explain that you are doing an investigation as part of your studies and you would be grateful if the person would agree to help. Try to be quite neutral about the information being given. It is not part of your job as an objective researcher to argue or disagree with people's points of view. You are there to find out their opinions, not to give your own.

If people seem reluctant to answer your questions even after you have politely explained what you are doing, don't pester them or pry into subjects which they don't want to discuss. This would be rudeness on your part.

Lastly, be sure to thank them for their help in completing the questionnaire or answering your questions.

Interpreting Your Results

When all the questionnaires are completed it will be time to sort out your results, to classify your sample, to count up the various ticks in coded choice answers, to make a note of interesting or typical or revealing comments in open-ended answers and to offer your interpretation of the total findings.

Coded choice answers can be totalled and made into percentages on tally sheets in the following way. Look again at the example question on p. 61, 'What are your main reasons for going to see a particular film?' *Eight* alternatives (a–h) are offered as possible answers. To interpret the results of this question asked of a sample of 100 people, set out your tally sheet like this:

Q. *What are your main reasons for going to see a particular film?*

	Total no. of mentions	Total no. in the sample	Percentage no. of mentions
a	9	100	9%
b	19	100	19%
c	13	100	13%
d	20	100	20%
e	8	100	8%
f	16	100	16%
g	10	100	10%
h	5	100	5%

By preparing similar tally sheets for each of your coded choice questions you can work out the trends in people's opinions and behaviour into percentages which will speak for themselves.

Writing a Report

The report that you write at the end of your investigation is the last task to complete in your research project. You should aim to make it fairly brief, a summary of all the ingredients in your research divided into sub-headed sections, together with your results, interpretation and conclusions, and any possible recommendations you want to make. An appendix at the end of the report could give full details of the statistical results which support your interpretations and conclusions. Here is a plan to help you:

1 Definition of the issue investigated

2 The particular aspects of the issue tested

3 How the sample was drawn up

4 Methods of investigation – e.g., Postal Questionnaire or Interview Questionnaire

5 How the information was collected and analysed

6 Results expressed either in writing or as graphs of percentages, together with quotes from open-ended answers

7 Your interpretation of the findings

8 Recommendations based on the results you collected

9 Appendix giving statistical tables in full

Discussion and Written Work

1 Because journalists write about social problems they often claim to be sociologists. Discuss the ways in which sociology is different from journalism.

2 Suggest the problems a sociologist would face joining a teenage gang to observe its behaviour.

3 Why are questionnaires more widely used than informal interviews in social research?

4 What would be the sampling frame you would use:
(a) To investigate attendance at a youth club?
(b) To study housing conditions in the area of the school?
(c) To analyse people's voting habits in local elections?

5 (a) Draw a random sample of pupils in the 4th Year.
(b) Draw a stratified sample of pupils in the school.
(c) Draw a systematic sample of members of staff in your school.

6 Provide the coded choice answers for the following questions:
(a) Why are examinations important?
(b) Which particular party did you support in the last election?
(c) Why do you play bingo here every evening?

7 Construct a short questionnaire on T.V. viewing habits consisting of three classifying questions, three factual questions, and three opinion questions.

8 Design a questionnaire of not more than twenty questions on a topical social issue of your own choosing.

9 Working as a class group:
(a) Devise a questionnaire on the T.V. viewing habits of teenagers worked out from Question 7.
(b) Draw up a sample of pupils.
(c) Test the questions in a pilot study.
(d) Give out the questionnaires to your sample.
(e) Collect and interpret the findings of the completed questionnaires.
(f) Write a report of the investigation using the plan on p. 63 to guide you.

Part Two

Homes and Families

Families are a Social Necessity

Can you imagine a situation in this country in which there were no families? How would people live? Do you think there would be great barracks and dormitories for people to share, or would each individual have his own tiny cell in a multi-storey apartment block?

When the children were produced, who would care for them until they were old enough to look after themselves? Who would teach them the behaviour of our society so that they understood what was right and wrong and what was normal and abnormal? Who would give them love and security in the years when their personality was developing and protect them in situations which they found distressing or confusing?

Without families, how would adults find permanent and secure social companionship with others? Who would tend them if they were ill, tolerate their moods and imperfections, and look after them when they were old? Could every individual provide enough money for his own needs without a family to share the responsibility? And what of those who could not work because they were too young, too old, or too ill?

Who would people go on holiday with, share meals with, tell secrets to, remember past happinesses with, and look forward to future plans with? Could all of these, and the hundred other daily ties which bind families together in a warm and intimate unit, be really shared with the stranger in the next dormitory or multi-storey living cell?

If you ask yourself these questions, it becomes clear that as a society we cannot do without the family. We could have good relationships with friends and allow the state to help with medical, welfare, and educational provisions, but all of these could only supplement the basic mutual dependence of the family group which rests on ties of blood and kinship.

Every country contains family units, but what is important to the sociologist is that these vary considerably between societies and differ noticeably even within societies. This proves that they are not so much a natural means of organisation as a social one.

Functions of the Family

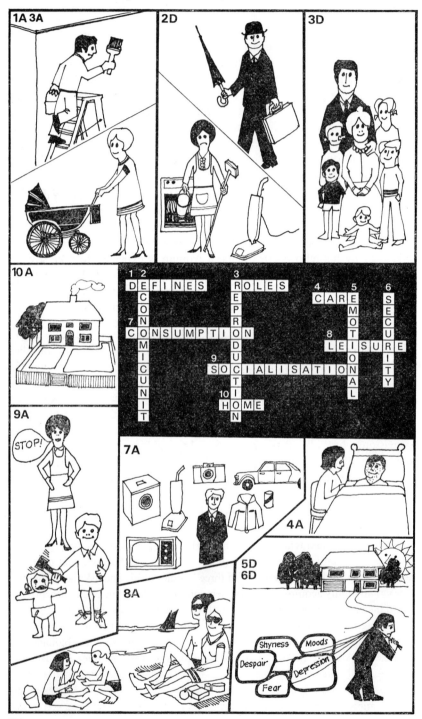

Chapter 5

Love and Marriage

One Mate or Many?

Any man in our society who tried to marry two women without a divorce separating the marriages would be breaking the laws of the land and most probably offending the consciences of his friends.

In some societies, however, the more wives a man has the more he is respected by his fellows. In others, a woman is expected to take several husbands, and those who do not are condemned as social failures. In some societies the very rich will have several wives, leaving insufficient to go round for the poor men. In these societies the women who are in scarce supply will each take two or more husbands to restore the balance.

The sociologist has special words for these kinds of relationships which you should learn:

1 Monogamy – marriage of one man to one woman.
2 Polygamy – marriage involving more than two partners:
(a) Polygyny – one man to two or more wives;
(b) Polyandry – one woman to two or more men.

Monogamy

Imagine a young American male in a romantic moonlight scene feeling very attracted to his girl. The customs and pressures of his society whisper very strongly in his ear, 'Marry, marry, marry', but he could of course do a number of things, as this quotation shows:

He could have sexual relations with the girl, leave, and never see her again. Or he could wait until her first child is born and then ask her maternal uncle to raise it. Or he could get together with three buddies of his and ask them whether they would jointly acquire the girl as their common wife. Or he could incorporate her in his harem along with the twenty-three females already living in it . . .

Having many wives, or being one of many husbands, is not a betrayal of humanity, in any biological sense, or even of virility. And since it is biologically possible for Arabs to have the one and for Tibetans to be the other, it must also be biologically possible for our young man. Indeed, we know that if the latter had been snatched out of his cradle and shipped to the right alien shores at an early enough age, he would not have grown up to be the red-blooded and more

69

than slightly sentimental all-American boy of our moonlight scene, but would have developed into a lusty polygamist in Arabia or a contented multiple-husband in Tibet. . .

From *Invitation to Sociology*, by Peter Berger

Polygamy

Each wife in a polygamus household has her own 'house' or establishment being made up of herself, her children and any other people inhabiting her compound. The compounds of the co-wives should normally be next to one another, or even joined together. But the actual arrangement seems to depend largely upon the wishes of the husband, and often enough the wives are placed some distance apart, although almost invariably within the same village.

While polygamy was an accepted practice with the Kgatla tribe of South Africa, it still gave rise to a certain jealousy among the women, as this account shows:

'I live with my wives very cleverly, I have handled them properly, so that they get on with each other. At first I had only one wife, and then I married a second named Mogatza. And when I found that Mogatza did not wish to live harmoniously with my senior wife, I slept only with the latter for many days in succession, without going to see Mogatza at all except in the afternoons. Then she said to me: "Why is it that you don't come into my blankets, did you marry me just to laugh at me?" And I replied, "Well, when I married you I did not say I was going to divorce my other wife". And she said, "If your senior wife does not want you to come to me, tell me and I shall know where to take the matter". Then I saw that this could lead to a serious quarrel, and so I said to her, "No, I am staying with that wife just to finish the month, then I shall come to you". Thereupon she was satisfied, and when the month was over I came to her, and began to sleep with her.

And it was also then that I took the medicine and secretly gave it to them both to drink, without their knowing what its purpose was. Since then there has been no trouble, they help each other at work, and they even eat together. I have laid down the rule that I shall sleep with each one for four days in succession, and then go to the other. I find them both equally desirable, but when I have slept with one for three days, by the fourth day she has wearied me, and when I go to the other I find that I have greater passion, she seems more attractive than the first, but it is not really so, for when I return to the latter again there is the same renewed passion'.

From *Married Life in an African Tribe*, by Isaac Schapero

Choosing a Mate

I expect you would be very angry if you could not marry the man or woman of your choice; the one you loved, the one you had courted, and the one you intended to spend your life with.

In many societies, however, young people have no such choice and do not know what is meant by 'falling in love'. Marriages are arranged for them by their parents, more or less as a business deal. Such marriages are usually planned in childhood or even before birth, and then the young people come together in their early teens. They often do not know very much about the appearance or personality of their partners and in many cases they have never even seen them.

Whatever type of marriage behaviour societies accept for themselves, it is important to remember that these exist as a result of past tradition and contemporary social pressure. The way in which young people behave has been taught to them by society from a very early age and hammered home by their family backgrounds, moral education, religion, and in industrial communities by the mass media and advertising.

Discussion and Written Work

1 (a) Give two examples of societies which practise:
   (i) monogamy
   (ii) polygyny
   (iii) polyandry
(b) Why is polyandry much less common than polygyny?

2 (a) Explain fully why arranged marriages are more common in pre-industrial societies than industrial societies.
(b) Do arranged marriages take place in Britain?

3 Consider together these accounts of being in love in three different societies, and then attempt the written work:

A. LONDON
One day or any day it is like this. I wait for my girl on Waterloo Bridge, and when she comes there is a mighty wind blowing across the river, and we lean against it and laugh, her skirt sky-larking, her hair whipping across her face.

I wooed my girl mostly on her way home from work, and I talked a great deal. Often it was as if I had never spoken; I heard my words echo in deep caverns of thought, as if they hung about like cigarette smoke in a still room, missionless; or else they were lost forever in the sounds of the city.

We used to wait for a 196 under a railway bridge across the Waterloo Road. There were always long queues and it looked like we would never get a bus.

71

Fidgeting in that line of impatient humanity I got in precious words edgeways, and a train would rumble and drown my words in thundering steel.

Still, it was important to talk. In the crowded bus, as if I wooed three or four instead of one, I shot words over my shoulder, across seats; once past a bespectacled man reading the Evening News, who lowered his paper and eyed me as if I was mad. My words bumped against people's faces, on the glass windows of the bus; they found passage between 'fares please' and once I got to writing things on a piece of paper and pushing my hand over two seats.

The journey ended and there was urgent need to communicate before we parted.

All these things I say, I said, waving my hand in the air as if to catch the words floating about me and give them mission. I say them because I want you to know, I don't ever want to regret afterwards that I didn't say enough; I would rather say too much.

From *My Girl and the City*, by Samuel Selvon

Write a piece in your own words to explain the feelings of the boy in the passage.

B. BUSHMEN OF THE KALAHARI

A Bushman, in love, carved a tiny little bow and arrow out of a sliver of the bone of a gemsbok, a great and noble animal with a lovely sweep of long crescent horn on its proud head. The bow was most beautifully made, about three inches long and matched with tiny arrows made out of stems of a sturdy grass that grew near water. The minute quiver was made from the quill of a giant bustard, the largest flying bird in the desert. The Bushman would stain the head of his arrows with a special potion and set out to stalk the lady of his choice. When he had done this successfully, he would shoot an arrow into her rump. If, on impact, she pulled out and destroyed the arrow, it was a sign that his courtship had failed. If she kept it intact, then it was proof that he had succeeded.

From *The Lost World of the Kalahari*, by Laurens Van der Post

Re-read the passage about Bushmen on pp. 46–50 then answer the following questions:
1 What skill did Bushmen society prize above all others?
2 What special knowledge of botany and chemistry was associated with this skill?
3 Explain the significance of the 'bow and arrow' and the 'special potion' in the Bushman's courtship behaviour.

C. TEPOZTLÁN, MEXICO

Today, courtship and the sending of love letters are common in the village, and few girls over thirteen or boys over fifteen do not have a sweetheart. The local priest has recognised this situation and has stated publicly that having a novio is not a sin and need not be mentioned in confession. A great deal of secrecy still surrounds courtship, however, and the girl still fears punishment.

As a first step in courting the boy sends the girl a letter declaring his love. Some boys may send several anonymous letters before they have the courage to sign their name. Boys with more education and self-confidence may initiate courtship in person by trying to detain the girl on the street. If the girl consents to let him walk by her side, he will at once propose that they be novios. It is a common sight to see a young boy loitering around a street corner for hours, waiting to get a glimpse of his novia or to say a few words to her. This 'cornering' of a girl is a regular courting practice in Tepoztlán. At nights boys often gather at a corner to play the guitar and serenade a nearby novia of one of the group.

Because of the difficulty in meeting, sending letters is a necessity after a boy and girl become novios. Letters may be left in a secret place or delivered by a trusted friend or child. Widows and girls may be hired for the purpose of delivering love messages, patching quarrels, or convincing a girl to become someone's novia. Known by the insulting terms of alcahuets or corre-ve-y-dile (run-see-and-tell), such go betweens are strongly disapproved of; they are also suspected of knowing how to use sorcery particularly appropriate for novios. Love magic may be resorted to if courting is difficult. Powdered bone from a human skull, placed in a girl's hand, in her hair, or in a sweet drink will make her fall in love. The leg of a beetle placed in a girl's drink will make her desire sexual relations. The use of sorcery for revenge by a jilted novia is very much feared by young men. The novia is believed to be able to make her former lover ill by sticking pins through a picture of him. Chronic illness in young men is often attributed to some girl's black magic.

Novios do not necessarily marry and may not have sexual relations. They generally caress and embrace but rarely kiss. Kissing is a modern innovation of courtship which only the more sophisticated have adopted. It is common today to have several novios before marriage, but a girl who has many novios, or who has them simultaneously, is called loca or crazy and severely criticised. A boy who has many novias is credited with being macho or manly but is not considered a desirable marriage partner.

From *Tepoztlán – Village in Mexico*, by Oscar Lewis

1 Explain in your own words the part played in Mexican courtship by:
(a) love letters
(b) go-betweens
(c) love magic
(d) kissing
2 Are there any ways in which you think the behaviour of young people in

Mexico is similar to that of young people in this country?
3 In what ways is their behaviour different to your own?
4 Read and discuss together these accounts of marriage in various societies, then attempt the written work:

A. NEW GUINEA
(Ngalen's marriage was arranged when she was 11 and during the 7 years of her engagement she was forbidden to think about or have any contact with her future husband.)

Ngalen is eighteen; for seven years she has been engaged to Manoi, whose very name is forbidden to her. She has seen him once as a very small child when her mother had taken her children to her own village of Peri. She remembers that he had a funny nose and a squint in one eye and had worn a bedraggled old *laplap*. But she has tried not to think of these things, for mother had taught her that it was shameful to think of her husband personally. She was forbidden to go to Peri, her mother's home village, except on very important occasions, like the death of a near relative. Then she must go about very circumspectly, wrapped in her mantle of cloth lest she encounter her betrothed's father or brother. If a Peri canoe passed her father's canoe at sea, she must hide within the pent-house or double up in the hull.

Her father is well pleased with the match. Ten thousand dogs' teeth will be paid, ten thousand dogs' teeth which he can very well use to pay for a wife for his brother's son who is turned fifteen and unbetrothed.

Her father and brothers go away and she is left alone with the women, who dye her hair red, paint her face and arms and back orange, wrap the long strands of shell about her limbs. Two heavy shell aprons are fastened under the breast-bands. In her arm-bands are hidden porcelain pipes, knives and forks and spoons, combs and small mirrors, the foreign property which is never used except to deck out a bride. A bristling coronet of dogs' teeth is fastened about her fore-head. Inside it are ranged a dozen tiny feather combs. Yards of trade cloth and bird of paradise feathers are stuck in her arm-bands. Her distended ear lobes are weighted down with extra clusters of dogs' teeth.

Like a rag doll she submits to the dressing process, meanwhile the women of her future husband's house have come to fetch her.

From *Growing Up in New Guinea*, by Margaret Mead

1 What is the purpose and significance of the Manus engagement?
2 What is the purpose and significance of the period of engagement in British courtship?
3 Explain *in your own words* how the Manus girl is dressed for her wedding.

74

4 Think very carefully about the preparations for the same ceremony in Britain. Imagine you had to describe this to a Manus audience and explain how an English bride is dressed for her wedding, commenting on the significance of her clothes and the part played by custom and tradition in her preparations.

B. CHINA

(Marriage in a Chinese village, if not actually arranged, is helped along by the young people's relatives.)

A person with a son over twenty and not yet married grows anxious lest his son becomes an old bachelor. He happens to have a relative in another village, who has a daughter who is not yet engaged, so the man takes his son and they go together to visit this relative. The boy and the girl cannot meet otherwise. Things are arranged so that the two can see each other, and afterwards they are asked: 'Did you like him?' 'Did you fall in love with her?' After that, the two young people meet again and perhaps they do fall in love, become engaged and get married. When Chang-Chung-liang's younger brother, Chang-Chung-wen, was twenty-two and still unmarried, he went to Chitan hsien, where he had an uncle, and his uncle introduced him to a very young girl. They got married and she now has a child of four, though she herself is only twenty-one.

When a girl considers the boys with an eye to choosing one to marry, she looks for one who is strong and healthy and able to work well. Girls attach great importance to behaviour: the boy they choose must be even- not quick-tempered. Appearance is less important. As the girls say: 'We have a long life to live together. He may look handsome, but his looks will soon go. But if he is faithful and kind and hard-working, we can have a good life together.' Boys who are known to be lazy seldom get married.

When a boy considers a girl, the first thing he asks himself is: 'Can she look after a home?' Next in importance is that she should be even-tempered. Appearance plays a certain part, but not a great one. In Liu Ling, no one will say that a girl is ugly or plain, just that she 'looks well enough in her way'.

In the towns the girls will tell you the same as those in the villages, but they will only do that because it is the thing to say. In reality, town girls want smart, dashing-looking boys.

The person with the most say in the matter of the girl's marriage is her grandmother, then her grandfather, then her mother: what her father thinks is of the least importance. What they all want for the girl they are marrying off – and what the boy's parents are also looking for – is a 'good marriage' to someone who is 'rich', strong and able to work well.

Once they are engaged, the boy and girl meet often. Li Chin-wa and Lo Han-hong spent hours sitting together in his cave. They were always alone then and no-one would disturb them. 'We aren't so feudal in Liu Ling that we won't leave them alone together.' But when Lo Han-hong goes to see Li Chin-wa, he has to sit with the whole family. Sometimes the two would go to the cinema in the town together.

There is no intercourse prior to marriage. That is held to be immoral. 'No girl in Liu Ling has ever had a baby before she was married. That very seldom happens up here with us in Northern Shansi.' The age at which girls normally marry is such that there is no large group of sexually mature but unmarried women.

Later on, when they are to marry, the two young people go to the Authorities and register. They have to say how old they are and they are asked: 'Do you love each other? Do you want to marry? Are you doing this of your own free will?' Only after that are they given a marriage licence.

From *Report from a Chinese Village*, by Jan Myrdal

1 Why do you think a willingness to 'work hard' is the main quality that both boys and girls in a Chinese village look for in a marriage partner?
2 (a) How concerned are the boys and girls about each other's looks?
(b) How important are 'good looks' in boy and girl relationships in Britain?
3 What does the fact that the girl's grandmother and grandfather have the most say in the marriage tell you about the social stratification of a Chinese village?

C. AMERICA
In the fifties came the revolutionary discovery of the teenage market. Teenagers and young marrieds began to figure prominently in the surveys. It was discovered that young wives, who had only been to high school and had never worked, were more 'insecure,' less independent, easier to sell. These young people could be told that, by buying the right things, they could achieve middle-class status, without work or study. The keep-up-with-the Joneses sell would work again; the individuality and independence which American women had been getting from education and work outside the home was not such a problem with the teenage brides. In fact, the surveys said, if the pattern of 'happiness through things' could be established when these women were young enough, they could be safely encouraged to go out and get a part-time job to help their husbands pay for all the things they buy. The main point now was to convince the teenagers that 'happiness through things' is no longer the prerogative of the rich or the talented; it can be enjoyed by all, if they learn 'the right way' the way the others do it, if they learn the embarrassment of being different.

In the words of one of these reports:
49% of these new brides were teenagers, and more girls marry at the age of 18 than at any other age. This early family formation yields a larger number of

young people who are on the threshold of their own responsibilities and decision-making in purchases. . .

But the most important fact is of a psychological nature: marriage today is not only the culmination of a romantic attachment; more consciously and more clearheadedly than in the past, it is also a decision to create a partnership in establishing a comfortable home, equipped with a great number of desirable products.

In talking to scores of young couples and brides-to-be, we found that, as a rule, their conversations and dreams centred to a very large degree around their future homes and their furnishings, around shopping 'to get an idea', around discussing the advantages and disadvantages of various products. . . .

The modern bride is deeply convinced of the unique value of married love, of the possibilities of finding real happiness in marriage and of fulfilling her personal destiny in it and through it.

But the engagement period today is a romantic, dreamy and heady period only to a limited extent. It is probably safe to say that the period of engagement tends to be a rehearsal of the material duties and responsibilities of marriage. While waiting for the nuptials, couples work hard, put aside money for definite purchases, or even begin buying on an instalment plan.

What is the deeper meaning of this new combination of an almost religious belief in the importance and beauty of married life on the one hand, and the product-centred outlook, on the other? . . .

The modern bride seeks as a conscious goal that which in many cases her grandmother saw as a blind fate and her mother as slavery: to belong to a man, to have a home and children of her own, to choose among all possible careers the career of wife-mother-homemaker.

From *The Feminine Mystique*, by Betty Friedan

While 'the revolutionary discovery of the teenage market' came to the Americans in the fifties, their sales pressure on this particular age group is even stronger today than it was then because of the improved techniques of their 20 years' experience of persuasion.

1 What kind of values is the advertising man trying to press upon teenage brides in America?
2 Why is it particularly easy to sell to these young brides?
3 What expectations of marriage do the majority of young American girls hold?
4 In what ways do their attitudes to marriage differ from those of their mothers and grandmothers?
5 Explain clearly how far you think the writer's interpretation of marriage could be applied to the marriages in this country. (Before you begin,

examine your own feelings on this. What sort of home do *you* want? When you are engaged, will you save most of your money at the expense of holidays and social outings? Would you marry on the spur of the moment with nothing planned, or would you want everything in your house to be ready to move into? Also, how important have a house and possessions been to young married couples you have known?)

D. 'THE GAMES PEOPLE PLAY'
When you have read the passage carefully, discuss the meanings of the words in italics before attempting the written work.

Our lives are not only dominated by the *inanities* of our contemporaries, but also by those of men who have been dead for generations. This is important to stress because it shows us that even in the areas where society apparently allows us some choice the powerful hand of the past narrows down this choice even further. Let us take for example, a scene in which a pair of lovers are sitting in the moonlight. Let us further imagine that this moonlight session turns out to be the decisive one, in which a proposal of marriage is made and accepted. They who are dead have long ago written the script for almost every move that is made. The notion that sexual attraction can be translated into romantic emotion was cooked up by misty-voiced minstrels *titillating* the imagination of aristocratic ladies about the twelfth century or thereabouts. The idea that a man should *fixate* his sexual drive permanently and exclusively on one single woman, with whom he is to share bed, bathroom and the boredom of a thousand bleary-eyed breakfasts, was produced by *misanthropic theologians* some time before that. And the assumption that the initiative in the establishment of this wondrous arrangement should be in the hands of the male, with the female graciously succumbing to the *impetuous onslaught* of his wooing, goes back right to prehistoric times when savage warriors first descended on some peaceful *matriarchal* hamlet and dragged away its screaming daughters to their marital cots.

Just as all these *hoary ancients* have decided the basic framework within which the passions of our exemplary couple will develop, so each step in their courtship has been predefined, prefabricated – if you like, 'fixed'. It is not only that they are supposed to fall in love and to enter into a monogamous marriage in which she gives up her name and he his *solvency*, but this love must be manufactured at all cost or the marriage will seem insincere to all concerned.

Each step in their courtship is laid down in *social ritual* also, and, although there is always some leeway for improvisations, too much *adlibbing* is likely to risk the success of the whole operation. In this way, our couple progresses predictably from movie dates to church dates to meeting-the-family dates, from holding hands to tentative explorations to what they originally planned to save for afterwards, from planning their evening to planning their suburban ranch house – with the scene in the moonlight put in its proper place in this *ceremonial sequence*. Neither of them has invented this game or any part of it. They have only decided that it is with each other, rather than with other possible partners, that they will play it. Family, friends, clergy, salesmen of jewelry and of life insurance, florists and interior decorators ensure that the remainder of the game will also be played by the established rules. Nor, indeed, do all these guardians of tradition have to exert much pressure on the principal players, since the expectations of their social world have long ago been built into their own *projections* of the future – they want precisely that which society expects of them.

From *Invitation to Sociology*, by Peter Berger

1 What two important influences principally affect the way we behave?

2 What are the three basic elements of the framework of Western marriage and in what historical circumstances did these originate?

3 (a) Explain in your own words the various stages in the social ritual of American courtship.

(b) Work out a similar scheme to show the typical stages of courtship for British teenagers.

4 Who else plays an influential part in the marriage game? Explain in each case the reasons why these people participate.

5 Do you feel that the young people are being manipulated ('pushed around') in any way? Give your reasons fully.

Chapter 6

Family Organisation

The Extended Family in Pre-Industrial Societies

The extended family is the usual pattern of family organisation in pre-industrial societies, where the whole kinship group is a social and economic unit, living probably in the same village, sharing work duties, responsibilities, and the fruits of production. Usually only enough is produced for the group's own needs, with perhaps a little left over for trade and special occasions. We call this hand to mouth existence a subsistence economy. The rate of social change in this type of society is very slow; each member of the family, from the eldest to the youngest, has a specific role to play and this is constantly reinforced by custom and tradition as the older generation initiates the new.

The Kgatla Tribe of South Africa

This tribe lives in extended family groups.

The household consists typically of a man with his wife or wives and dependent children, but often includes other people as well. It may be a simple biological family, or comprise two or more which are very closely related. Members of the same household associate together more intimately than the members of any other group in the tribe. They live, eat, work and play together, consult and help one another in all personal difficulties, and share in one another's good fortune. They produce the great bulk of their own food and other material wants; they form a distinct legal and administrative unit under their own head; they are the group within which children are born, reared and trained in conduct and methods of work; and they perform the ceremonies connected with birth, marriage, death and other ritual occasions. The self-contained character of the household appears most strongly perhaps at the fields, where for part of the year it lives as an isolated unit. In structure it tends to be of the *patriarchal type*, in that a wife normally lives with her husband among his paternal relatives, and, with her children, is legally under his authority, while succession, descent and inheritance of property, are all *patrilineal* . . .

Each household normally produces the great bulk of its domestic requirements. It gets its food by cultivating Kafir corn and other crops, breeding livestock, hunting, and collecting wild edible plants. Deficits are made good by gifts or loans from relatives or friends, or by exchange for some other commodity, but nobody ever obtains all or even most of his food in this way. Each household also builds its own huts and granaries, and does its own housework. In all these activities everybody except the infants take part, men, women and children, having specified occupations according to sex and age. The women and girls till the fields, build and repair the walls of the huts, granaries and courtyard, prepare food and make beer, look after the fowls, fetch water, wood and earth, collect wild plants and do all the other housework. The men and boys herd the cattle and small stock, hunt, and do all the timber-work in building. Tasks that a household is too small to carry out for itself, or wishes to complete more rapidly than is possible working alone, are generally done either with the aid of relatives, or by organizing a work-party and paying with meat, beer or some similar commodity, the neighbours coming to help. Poor people have no other means of getting sufficient labour for such big undertakings as clearing or weeding a field, threshing corn, or building a hut; and since they are accordingly all dependent upon one another, it is good policy to help others when invited. The only specialist doing work for which most households are not equipped is the magician, whose services have to be hired for the protective and beneficient doctoring of compounds, fields and cattle-posts.

From *Married Life in an African Tribe*, by Isaac Schapera

Manus Family Life

In Manus society marriages are arranged and relatives live together in extended family groups:

The relationship between husband and wife is usually strained and cold. The blood-ties with their parents are stronger than their relationship to each other, and there are more factors to pull them apart than to draw them together.

The bridegroom has no attitude of tenderness or affection for the girl whom he has never seen before the wedding. She fears her first sex experience as all the women of her people have feared and hated it. No foundation is laid for happiness on the wedding night, only one for shame and hostility. The next day the bride goes about the village with her mother-in-law to fetch wood, and water. She had not yet said one word to her husband.

This sense that husband and wife belong to different groups persists throughout the marriage, weakening after the marriage has endured for many years, never vanishing entirely. The father, mother, and children do not form a warm intimate unit, facing the world. In most cases the man lives in his own village, in his own part of the village, near his brothers and uncles. Near by will live some of his sisters and aunts. These are the people with whom all his ties are closest, from whom he has learned to expect all his rewards since childhood. These are the people who fed him when he was hungry, nursed him when he was sick, paid his fines when he was sinful, and bore his debts for him. Their spirits are his spirits, their taboos his taboos. To them he has a strong sense of belonging.

But his wife is a stranger. He did not choose her; he never thought of her before marriage without a sense of shame. Before he married her he was free in his own village at least. He could spend hours in the men's house, strumming and singing. Now that he is married, he cannot call his soul his own. All day long he must work for those who paid for his wedding. He must walk shame-facedly in their presence, for he has discovered how little he knows of the obligations into which he is plunged. He has every reason to hate his shy, embarrassed wife, who shrinks with loathing from his rough, unschooled embrace and has never a good word to say to him. They are ashamed to eat in each other's presence. Officially they sleep on opposite sides of the house. For the first couple of years of marriage, they never go about together.

The girl's resentment of her position does not lessen with the weeks. These people are strangers to her. To them her husband is bound by the closest ties their society recognizes. If she is away from her people, in another village, she tries harder than does her husband to make something of her marriage. If the bride has married in her own village, she goes home frequently to her relatives and makes even less effort at the hopeless task of getting along well with her husband. For her marriage her face was tattooed, her short curly hair was dyed red. But now her head is clean shaven and she is forbidden to ornament herself. If she does, the spirits of her husband will suspect her of wishing to be attractive to men and will send sickness upon the house. She may not even gossip, softly, to a female relative about her husband's relatives. The spirits who live in the skull-bowls will hear her and punish. She is a stranger among strange spirits, spirits who nevertheless exercise a rigid espionage over her behaviour.

When she conceives, she is drawn closer, not to the father of her child, but to her own kin. She may not tell her husband that she is pregnant. Such intimacy would shame them both. Instead, she tells her mother and her father, her sisters and her brothers, her aunts and her cross-cousins. Her relatives set to work to prepare the necessary food for the pregnancy feasts. Still nothing is said to the husband. Then some chance word reaches his ears, some rumour of the economic preparations his brothers-in-law are making. Still he cannot mention the point to his wife, but he waits for the first feast when canoes laden with sago come to his door. The months wear on, marked by periodic feasts for which he must make repayment. His relatives help him, but he is expected to do most of it himself. He must go to his sisters' houses and beg them for beadwork. His aunts and mother must be asked to help. He is constantly worried for fear his repay-ments will not be enough, will not be correctly arranged. Meanwhile his pregnant wife sits at home making yards of beadwork for her brothers, working for her brothers while he must beg and cajole his sisters.

A few days before the birth of the child the brother or cousin or uncle of the expectant mother divines for the place of birth. The divination declares whether the child shall be born in the house of its father or of its maternal uncle. If the former is the verdict, the husband must leave his house and go to his sister's. His brother-in-law and his wife and children move into his house. Or else his wife is taken away sometimes to another village. From the moment her labour begins he may not see her. The nearest approach he can make to the house is to bring fish to the landing-platform. For a whole month he wanders aimlessly about, sleeping now at one sister's, now at another's. Only after his brother-in-law has worked or collected enough sago, one or two tons at least, to make the return feast, can his wife return to him, can he see his child.

Now begins a new life. The father takes a violent proprietary interest in the new baby. It is his child, belongs to his kin, is under the protection of his spirits. He watches his wife with jealous attention, scolds her if she stirs from the house, shouts at her if the baby cries. He can be rougher with her now. The chances are that she will not run away, but will stay where her child will be well cared for. For a year mother and baby are shut up together in the house. For that year the child still belongs to its mother. The father only holds it occasionally, is afraid to take it from the house. But as soon as the child's legs are strong enough to stand upon and its small arms adept at clutching, the father begins to take the child from the mother. Now that the child is in no need of such frequent suckling, he expects his wife to get to work, to go to the mangrove swamp to work sago, to make long trips to the reef for shell-fish. She has been idle long enough, for, say the men, 'a woman with a new baby is no use to her husband, she cannot work'. The plea that her child needs her would not avail. The father is delighted to play with the child, to toss it in the air, tickle it beneath its armpits, softly blow on its bare smooth skin. He has risen at three in the morning to fish, he has fished all through the cold dawn, punted the weary way to market, sold some of his fish for good bargains in taro, in betel nut, in taro leaves. Now he is free for the better part of the day, drowsy, just in the mood to play with the baby.

Father is obviously the most important person in the home; he orders mother about, and hits her if she doesn't 'hear his talk'. Father is even more indulgent than mother. It is a frequent picture to see a little minx of three leave her father's arms, quench her thirst at her mother's breast, and then swagger back to her father's arms, grinning overbearingly at her mother. The mother sees the child drawn further and further away from her. At night the child sleeps with the father, by day she rides on his back. He takes her to the shady island which serves as a sort of men's club house where all the canoes are built and large fish-traps made. Her mother can't come on this island except to feed the pigs when no men are there. Her mother is ashamed to come there, but she can rollick gaily among the half-completed canoes. When there is a big feast, her mother must hide in the back of the house behind a hanging mat. But she can run away to father in the front of the house when the soup and betel nut are being given out. Father is always at the centre of interest, he is never too busy to play. Mother is often busy. She must stay in the smoky interior of the house. She is forbidden the canoe islands. It is small wonder the father always wins the competition: the dice are loaded from the start.

On the eve of the birth of a new baby, the child's transfer of dependence to its father is almost complete. While the mother is occupied with her new baby, the older child stays with its father. He feeds it, bathes it, plays with it all day. He has little work or responsibility during this period and so more time to strengthen his position. This repeats itself for the birth of each new child. The mother welcomes birth; again she will have a baby which is her own, if only for a few months. And at the end of the early months the father again takes over the younger child. Occasionally he may keep a predominant interest in the older child, especially if the older is a boy, the younger a girl, but usually there is room in his canoe for two or three little ones. And the elder ones of five and six are not pushed out of the canoe, they leave it in the tiny canoes which father has hewn for them. At first upset, the first rebuff, they can come swimming back into the sympathetic circle of the father's indulgent love for his children.

From *Growing Up in New Guinea*, by Margaret Mead

Manus Economy

Their economic system was one of the most elaborate of primitive systems for which we have any record. They had real money. Dogs' teeth and shell beads, as handled by them, met all the requirements of a modern definition of money. But there was no dependence upon a monetary system to ensure the manufacture of the objects that people needed. There was reliance instead on a kind of compulsory barter, fish for tubers and sago, lime for the betel nut and pepper leaves. Each trader compelled others to bring him, either to the market or in terms of individual trade friendship, the particular objects which he needed. Barter was the rule – one kind of desired object in return for another kind of desired object, without dependence upon money to stimulate the necessary production.

Within a Manus village, there was a day-to-day, hand-to-mouth subsistence economy. It was necessary that someone from every household should fish, daily, nightly, to trade for fresh supplies of taro, pepper leaf and betel nut, and to supply their own pots.

This was the system through which the daily supply of food was brought in by the daily toil of fishermen – matching the daily toil of land people as gardeners and sago workers – and the system in which unremitting industry, planning, scheming, trading, sailing, combined with the tireless handiwork of the women – stringing and combining beads and rubber nut into ornaments, bark into cloth and string, leaves into thatch, clay into pots – made possible the provision of the materials for the more permanent needs of life.

In Manus, differences in wealth and ability were compensated for by two devices. In the first place, there was no system of communal responsibility through which the lazy and inefficient could escape doing their share. In the great exchanges where hundreds of thousands of dogs' teeth changed hands, each individual's contribution and responsibility were graded and people who could not meet big debts acquired only small credits. The second device was that the more successfully a man conducted his affairs, the more he was impelled to undertake.

This system ensured that the rich and enterprising were punished if they paused for a moment in pursuing their farflung enterprises, and that the man who had elected to remain a dependent of some entrepreneur was chastised for not fulfilling his simple dependent role.

From *New Lives for Old*, by Margaret Mead

Discussion and Written Work

1 (a) What are the main functions of the Kgatla extended family?

(b) Discuss the meanings and significance of the two words *patriarchal* and *patrilineal* italicised in Extract 1 on p. 80.

(c) Make a list of men's jobs and women's jobs in the Kgatla household.

(d) In this division of labour, who is responsible for doing the most work?

(e) What name do we give to the Kgatla type of economic system?

(f) On what sort of relationship between people does this type of economic system depend? Give three examples from the passage to support your answer.

(g) What was the only specialist task in which the households were not sclf-sufficient?

(h) Describe *in your own words* the job of this specialist.

2 (a) Write a description of the type of society in which the Manus people live, using these headings:

    (i) geographical features

    (ii) the work of the people

    (iii) religious beliefs

    (iv) food and clothing

(b) The young man hasn't chosen a girl whom he loves to marry. Explain how and why the marriage has come about.

(c) How does the husband's relationship with his wife compare with his relationship to his family?

(d) What duties does the husband owe to those who paid for his wedding?

(e) Describe *in your own words* the wife's relationship to her husband and to his family.

85

(f) Why must she be careful of the 'spirits who live in the skull bowls'?

(g) What happens when the wife finds out she is going to have a child?

(h) Explain what happens to the relationship between husband and wife when the child is born.

(i) Explain what kind of relationship exists between
    (i) the child and its mother
    (ii) the child and its father

(j) From what you have learned about Manus family life, write an essay to explain the main ways in which it differs from our own.

3 (a) What name is given to the type of economy practised in Manus society?

(b) Explain in your own words the way in which the economic system of the Manus works.

(c) How does the society ensure that everyone plays his part?

The Extended Family in Industrial Societies
The extended family is also a term which has been used to describe British working class life in the older areas of industrial cities. Here members of the same family live in close co-operation with relatives, sharing each other's lives in a way which is not true of the more independent family units of mother, father and children, living separate existences on new estates or in suburban areas.

Discuss together these examples:

A. MRS LYONS
Mrs Lyons, a widow of sixty-eight, lived with her married daughter, son-in-law, and four grandchildren. She did the cooking, bathed the baby and the next youngest child, and looked after the baby when her daughter went to collect two other children from school. Her daughter said, 'It helps me really, having her. She keeps an eye on the children for me.' And she added, as if her mother had a proper and rightful share in the children's world, 'My husband likes messing about in the garden . . . I don't like leaving her on her own.' The daughter did all the shopping, managed the household and, in partnership with her mother, attended to the children, besides working four hours a day as a machinist.

B. MRS RILK
Mrs Rilk, an infirm widow in her early sixties, lived alone. A married daughter living nearby regularly did her cleaning and gave her meals on Sundays. Her shopping was done by a thirteen-year-old grandson. 'He comes every morning before school.' As for washing, another grandson 'calls in when he's on his milk round on Sunday and collects it. My daughter gets it done on a Monday and

Charlie [the grandson] brings it back.' Her grandchildren chopped firewood for her, exercised her dog and took her to the cinema or to the bus-stop. Her daughter collected the pension. But Mrs Rilk prepared a meal for her daughter and grandchildren six days of the week, often entertained her relatives in the evenings, and once or twice a week she took a meal to an old lady in the same block of flats.

C. MRS KNOCK

Mrs Knock, aged sixty-four, lived with her husband, a single son, and a grand-daughter of six years old. Her eldest daughter lived in the next street and her youngest daughter in the same street. She saw them and their children every day. They helped her with the shopping and she looked after the grandchildren when they were at work. Money was exchanged for these services. Her youngest son, recently married, lived two streets away and called every evening. Her two daughters had the midday meal with her and she sent a meal to her youngest son because his wife was at work in the day.

From *The Family Life of Old People*, by Peter Townsend

D. WORKING TOGETHER IN BETHNAL GREEN

The overwhelming majority of Bethnal Green men are manual workers, with a particularly high proportion of unskilled people. It is worth noting, too, that the professional classes are not like those elsewhere. The local government officers, teachers, doctors, welfare workers, and managers of the borough do not, on the whole, live within its borders. They travel in to their work every morning from outside. More than half of the 'white-collar' people in our general sample actually living in Bethnal Green were shopkeepers and publicans, in many ways more akin to the working-class people they serve than to the professional men and administrators with whom they are classified. The tone of the district is set by the working class.

Since they have similar jobs, the people also have much in common. They have the same formal education. They usually reach their maximum earnings at the age of twenty-one and stay at that level, unless all wages advance, for the rest of their lives. Though wages may vary from £8 to £20 a week, they are nearly all paid by the hour. They are no more secure than other hour-paid employees, liable to be dismissed without notice and deprived of pay during sickness, and, to counter insecurity, they have built the same trade union and political organizations.

Since relatives often have the same kind of work, they can sometimes help each other to get jobs. They do this in the same way as they get houses for each other – by putting in a good word in the right quarter – and reputation counts for one as much as for the other. A mother with a record of always being prompt with the rent has a good chance of getting a house for a daughter; a father with a record of being a good workman has a good chance of getting a job for his son, or indeed for any other relative he may recommend.

People get news all the time from their relatives about the jobs with better pay, better conditions, or more overtime, and their comparisons may induce men to change. 'I got my present job as a lorry driver through my brother-in-law,' said Mr Little. 'At that time I used to work for Blundells and he came down there and saw me. I was shifting big sacks about and he said, "Blimey, do you have to move these sacks by hand? You don't have to do that. Why don't you come over to us? There's none of that lark down there." So I went down to see them and got a job with them.'

In the docks, the markets, and in printing the right to family succession has been formally acknowledged. There are plenty of other examples in the district too, especially where there was heritable property – of shops where 'Brown & Son' meant what it said, of newspaper sellers who had inherited their 'pitches', of costermongers who had worked with their families because, in a business where confidence is essential, they did not have enough faith in anyone else.

Wherever father works with son and brother with brother, family and work-place are intertwined. When there is a quarrel at work, it spreads over into the family.

'My husband went to work for his brother Jim. Jim was a foreman scaffolder. Once when I was in hospital with a burnt hand, he came to see me and was late for work. Jimmy told him off and they had a tiff over it. My husband left and branched off on his own and we never see Jimmy any more.'

And where there is harmony at work it also spreads over into the family. Men who work with fathers or with brothers naturally see them every weekday, and often see a good deal of them when off work as well. Mr Aves, for instance, not content to work alongside two brothers and a brother-in-law in the same small building firm, sees them continuously at week-ends too.

'I see one of my brothers every Saturday at football, and then every Sunday the whole family comes down for a drink on Sunday morning. They've always done it. The men, my brothers and brothers-in-law, go round to the pub and then the women get the dinner cooked and come round for the last half hour for a chat and a drink. Oh, it's a regular thing in our family.'

From *Family and Kinship in East London*, by Young and Willmott

E. THE FISHERMAN'S FAMILY IN HULL

For three-quarters of her days the fisherman's wife is apart from her husband. Her main preoccupation is usually children and she is likely to have a slightly larger family than those of other working-class women. For instance, in sixty fishing families where the husband was in his thirties, the average number of children was over three – and many of the wives would, of course, later have more children.

While he is at sea the fisherman arranges for a regular weekly amount of money to be sent to his wife. The man can choose any amount he likes but any fisherman who allots his wife less than the whole of his basic wage is likely to become an object of derision to his mates. Many men allot their wives as much as £10 per week. In addition, husbands tend to buy substantial items like furniture and children's clothing.

A fisherman's wife, therefore, tends to be slightly better off than her neighbour – particularly since she does not have to feed her husband for a large part of the time. That she has comparatively more money than her neighbours, and probably more children, both contribute to the fact that few fishermen's wives go out to work.

The fishermen themselves are invariably against their wives working. When ashore, a fisherman likes to have all his meals cooked by his wife, and since his turn-round time between trips is more often than not in the middle of the week, this alone prevents his wife going out to work. But even in the fish processing houses, which are often willing to let women come and go very casually, and would not object to a woman taking three days off every three weeks, few fishermen's wives are found at work. Fishermen often think it is an insult to their capacity, or perhaps to their status as men, if their wives go out to work. What is the point of his sacrifice, his willingness to go fishing and to accept its hardships in order to get money, if his wife then decides to go out to work as well? Fishermen say quite frankly that they are jealous of their wives going out and meeting men – which would of course happen at work. Similarly, most fishermen while at sea discourage their wives from going out in the evenings. They are often critical too of the extent to which their wives visit their own mothers. But they accept mothers-in-law at worst as a necessary evil.

When her husband is at sea the wife needs understanding, companionship, help with her children, and a chance of escaping sometimes from what is otherwise the prison of her home. In the majority of cases these needs are satisfied by her mother. It seems to be usually only when the mother is dead, or does not live in Hull, or herself goes out to work, that the woman has to turn to a sister, perhaps, or a neighbour. When the woman's own family begin to grow up – especially when her eldest daughter is old enough to help in the house and to become a female gossip-partner – she may see less of her mother; although fishermen's wives are far from neglectful when their mother's help in domestic tasks is no longer required. Without exception, every fisherman's wife I interviewed, who had at least two children under ten years of age, and a mother alive in Hull, saw the mother regularly.

The fisherman's wife organizes her life around the task of bringing up her children – and this inevitably becomes in many ways more important than her other main task of looking after her husband during the ninety days or so each year when he is ashore.

The fisherman remains something of a stranger to his children. Men at sea talk a good deal about their 'bairns' but the attitude seems disinterested and more like that of an uncle than a father. Some men try to compensate for their absence by giving lavish presents to their children. One fisherman, complaining he was seldom home, said: 'The wife told me not long ago that my little daughter asked, "Mummy, who's that man who comes to stay with us?"'

During the last decade fishermen made up about $2\frac{1}{2}\%$ of the working men of Hull and East Riding, but accounted for about 5% of the divorces. This is hardly surprising in view of the strains inevitably imposed on the fisherman's marriage.

In many cases, it seems to be at the beginning of (or immediately before) the marriage that the conflict between the man and the woman is greatest. The fisherman does not usually have many interests in common with his wife. Some men quickly come to regard their wives merely as providers of sexual and cooking services, in return for a weekly wage. With the passage of time, however, conflict tends to be reduced.

Among fishermen a rough agreement exists as to what is reasonable behaviour for a fisherman in his marriage. It is widely believed that during a turn-round time of three days between trips, a man should spend some time with his wife apart from eating and sleeping with her. On the other hand it is regarded as unusual for a fisherman to spend all three evenings with his wife. Men who only go out drinking when accompanied by their wives tend to regard themselves as unusually virtuous.

Strain is exerted on the marriage by the contrast between what happens when a fisherman has three days' turn-round time and when he has three weeks or more out of a ship. Wives say that a husband, who the last time home spent £40 in three days, now begs for money to buy cigarettes.

Fishing homes usually show evidence of recent decorating, painting, wallpapering – and wives usually report that this has been done by the man. Most fishermen find themselves doing such jobs, behaving indeed like the prototype 'companion' husband. But even though many fishermen at such times adopt more humble roles in the home, it seems to be during these periods that conflict really develops. We have already seen that when a fisherman comes home he disrupts the normal routine. At first this is welcome, he comes bearing gifts for the children. His coming is the main event by which the passage of time in the home is marked, he brings the family into focus.

The fisherman's marriage is shaped by his occupation. The very sequence of his presence and absence is determined by his trawler trips. But also his marriage comes to shape his attitude to work. The motives which sent a boy fishing in the first place are different from those which continue to make a man go fishing in later years. These motives are inevitably bound up with his marriage. After he has been ashore a while the fisherman feels that certain pressures are being exerted on him to go back. Money is shorter. 'Dole and rebate' usually is only roughly the same as the weekly 'wage' the wife receives when he is at sea, and the total sum declines progressively. The man inevitably finds himself differently regarded by his wife after a week or two from how she regarded him after a day or two.

As he goes back to sea again he cannot help feeling that these two things – the smaller amount of cash and his wife's different attitude – are suspiciously closely related. Does the wife only want him when he has money? When he is there more than a few days why does she grow weary of him? Why is he going to sea just to pay that ungrateful wife and her children? 'Legalised prostitution.' One sees the point and it explains why fishermen say so often and so savagely that women are just 'money-grabbing bitches' and less polite things. 'My wife is all "Gimme, Gimme",' one man commented.

The consequences of his marriage feed back into the structure of the industry a number of important implications. Though the fisherman may give more than just his basic wage to his wife, there still remains the belief that the basic wage is hers and the rest is his. This is why the fisherman says that his pay has never been put up for years. (The poundage payment between 1947 and 1960 has changed only from 11s. 6d. to 12s. 9d. per £100 of the catch's auction price.) If you point out that the basic rate has gone up a number of times the fisherman says that the basic goes to his wife.

Thus fishermen come to distrust increases in the basic, and might distrust even more a large negotiated increase in the basic rates to compensate a drop in the poundage. In this way attitudes to pay, which are shaped in the context of the family, carry over into the field of trade unionism and labour-management relations.

From *The Fishermen*, by J. Tunstall

Discussion and Written Work

1 Why is the term 'extended family' applied to British working class living patterns?

2 Give examples from the passages to show the ways in which members of an extended family often help each other.

3 (a) Why do people who work in Bethnal Green have a great deal in common?
(b) Explain *in your own words* the part played by relatives in helping to get jobs.
(c) Working together with relatives has what effects on family life?

(d) What effects do you think these will have upon menfolk of extended families working together:

    (i) improved educational opportunities?

    (ii) the changes brought about by automation?

4 (a) What type of fishermen are referred to in the extract on pp. 88–91?

(b) Why is fishing a hard life for the men who go to sea?

(c) What do you know about the pay and working conditions of fishermen?

(d) Why are fishermen's wives usually 'better off' than their neighbours? Give examples of the ways in which they spend their extra money.

(e) Why don't fishermen like their wives to work?

(f) Some wives do go out to work. What special arrangements do local employers make to help them?

(g) Why do fishermen not like to think of their wives going out while they are away at sea?

(h) Why is the fisherman's wife's relationship with her mother particularly close?

(i) Why are fishermen's children likely to be spoilt or badly behaved?

(j) Give as many reasons as you can to explain why the divorce rate in fishermen's marriages is fairly high.

(k) What sort of behaviour is typical of the three days at home between trips?

(l) When a fisherman is at home for longer (say two or three weeks) why do strains in his relationship with his wife often develop?

(m) Imagine a man who works in a factory and lives on a new housing estate. Explain carefully in what ways you would expect his family life to be different from that of the fisherman. Use the following headings to help you: pay; working hours and conditions; living area; leisure activities; relationship with his wife; relationship with his children; relationship with relatives.

The Nuclear Family

The spread of industrialisation and the movement towards a much more complex city-life existence has meant that the dependence on a subsistence agricultural economy and the working together of the kinship group have both broken down. Family groups tend to become much smaller affairs, not so many children are produced, and the relationships centre more on the home than on the kinship community. These smaller family units, consisting of husband, wife, and two or three children living a separate existence, in contact with relatives but not in inter-dependence with them, are called nuclear families.

You have seen how extended families in Britain still exist in the old working class areas of industrial towns where their frequent lack of money, insecurity of employment, and closely-shared backgrounds and life-experiences have held the extended family unit together. As these areas are pulled down and the people are rehoused, or as increasing educational opportunity gives the young ambitions to go further afield, the old organisation is broken and is replaced by the development of the nuclear family.

Bethnal Green and Greenleigh

In their book, *Family and Kinship in East London*, Willmot and Young have painted a very vivid picture of the extended family life of the working class in London's East End. As the people of Bethnal Green are rehoused on Greenleigh Estate, twenty miles out of London, however, their kinship ties change:

That busy, sociable life is now a memory. Shopping in the mornings amidst the chromium and the tiles of the Parade is a lonely business compared with the familiar faces and sights of the old street market. The evenings are quieter too: 'It's the television most nights and the garden in the summer'. Mrs Harper knew no one when she arrived at Greenleigh, and her efforts to make friends have not been very successful. 'I tried getting friendly with the woman next door but one', she explained, 'but it didn't work.' It is the loneliness she dislikes most – and the 'quietness' which she thinks will in time 'send people off their heads'. . . .

Mrs Harper seldom sees her relatives any more. She goes to Bethnal Green only five or six times a year, when one of her elder sisters organises a family party 'for Dad'. 'It costs so much to travel up there', she said, 'that I don't recognise some of the children, they're growing up so fast.' Tired of mooching around an empty house all day, waiting for her husband and children to return, with no one to talk to and with the neighbours 'snobbish' and 'spiteful', Mrs Harper has taken a part-time job. 'If I didn't go to work, I'd get melancholic.' Her verdict on Greenleigh – 'It's like being in a box to die out here.'

Mrs Harper's story shows how great can be the change for a woman who moves from a place where the family is linked to relatives, neighbours, and friends in a web of intimate relationships to a place where she may talk to no one, apart from the children, from the moment her husband leaves for work in the morning until he comes home again, tired out by the journey, at seven or eight at night. It is not just that she sees less of relatives than before: as a day-to-day affair, as something around which her domestic economy is organised, her life arranged, the extended family has ceased to exist. . . .

In Bethnal Green, people with relatives close by seldom go short of money in a crisis. If they do not belong to a family club from which they can borrow a loan, some relatives will lend them money. Borrowing from relatives is often more difficult at Greenleigh. 'You notice the difference out here', said Mr Tonks, 'when you fall on hard times. Up there you were where you were born. You could always get helped by your family. You didn't even have to ask them – they'd help you out of trouble straight away. Down here you've had it. . . .'

The question about help at childbirth showed the same decline in dependence on relatives. The kindred of Bethnal Green were no longer predominant. Out of the 29 wives in Bethnal Green helped by relatives at their confinement, 18 were helped by their mothers: out of 19 at Greenleigh only one wife was – the Mrs Chortle whose mother lives with her. Of the remaining three relatives, two were living at Greenleigh, and one came out to stay. Of the other 15 families, neighbours helped only 5; one family turned to a Home Help; 7 husbands stayed off work; and in 2 families the children looked after themselves.

In day-to-day affairs, too, the neighbours rather rarely took the place of kin. A few wives said they went to the shops with another woman, or that they got errands for each other, or that they took turns at fetching the children from school. The most usual reaction was like that of Mrs Todd, who complained, 'When the baby was ill, not a soul knocked at my door to get me an errand.' Even where neighbours were willing to assist, people were apparently reluctant to depend on them too much or confide in them too freely. . . .

Husbands not only do more to aid their wives in emergencies; they also spend less on themselves and more on their families. When they watch the television instead of drinking beer in the pub, and weed the garden instead of going to a football match, the husbands of Greenleigh have taken a stage further the partnership characteristic of modern families. The 'home' and the family of marriage becomes the focus of a man's life, as of his wife's, far more completely than in the East End. 'You lose contact with parents and relations when you move out here,' said Mr Curtis. 'You seem to centre yourself more on the home. Everybody lives in a little world of their own.'

From *Family and Kinship in East London*, by Young and Willmott

The Nuclear Family in America
Several trends which may be accentuated by this present style of nuclear family organisation are being recognized: the plight of the half-educated woman whose children are already grown, the high male death rate in middle age, the aimless lives of older women, with neither husbands nor children to care for, the isolation of the divorced or widowed mothers of young children. In summary, it may be said that the division of roles between the sexes and the generations in the United States has undergone a profound change, with a focus upon very young marriage, early parenthood, and emotional self-sufficiency of each such unit, isolated in suburbia, strenuously seeking a romantic realization of a glamorous dream. This turning in upon the home for all satisfaction, with a decrease in friendship, in community responsibility, in work and creativeness, seems to be a function of the uncertainty about the future which is characteristic of this

generation. The care of very young infants by their fathers is something that no former civilization has encouraged among their educated and responsible men. Delight in motherhood has been recognized as a principal barrier to women's creativeness in work, but there is now added the danger that delight in parenthood may prove equally seductive to young men.

From *Male and Female*, by Margaret Mead

Family Changes in Kgatla Society

Christianity, modernisation and the impact of western civilisation has had a tremendous effect on the traditional culture of the Kgatla tribe of South Africa. But in the process of beneficial social change which these influences encouraged, many of the time-honoured traditions of the Kgatla gave way to new patterns of behaviour and the introduction of new social problems, as this passage shows:

Marriage and the family have been affected by the changing society with the result that the traditional structure of domestic life has been altered. Polygamy has become so exceptional that perhaps only one married man in thirty has two wives or more. But an important consequence has been the spread of concubinage. Many men now have mistresses whom formerly they might have married. This means that the children of these unions are illegitimate. It means also that wives have greater cause for jealousy, so that quarrels due to sexual infidelity have become a fairly common feature of married life. The relations between parents and children have also changed. Formerly children were wholly subject to their parents whom they had to obey without hesitation or question. They could not choose their own mates, but had to marry the people selected for them. Today, however, there is ample evidence of youthful irresponsibility and independence. Children no longer look always to their parents for approval, but are tending more and more to act as they please. Many of them now do their own courting, and infant betrothal, a recognized practice in old days, has almost entirely disappeared. Premarital sex relations, formerly severely condemned, have become almost a matter of course, and many girls bear children out of wedlock.

From *Married Life in an African Tribe*, by Isaac Schapera

Discussion and Written Work

1 (a) Describe the way of life of a nuclear family recorded by Willmott and Young in Greenleigh.
(b) Mr Curtis says, 'You seem to centre yourself more on the home. Everybody lives in a little world of their own.' Explain with examples the ways in which the mass media, and especially the advertising man, uses this home centredness as a means of creating values and selling products.

Here are some well-worn phrases to help you with your discussion: Your ideal home; Keeping up with the Joneses; What is a Mum? – Someone who cares enough to buy them . . . ; The breadwinner; The Englishman has a privet-hedge mentality; An Englishman's home is his castle; What will the neighbours say?; Your children *deserve* the best; Look after Number One; Life's a rat race; 'Love is said in many ways. It's giving and accepting. It's protecting and selecting . . . knowing what's safest for those you love. Their toilet tissue is Scott always. . . . Now in four colours and white.'

2 (a) In what way has family organisation in America changed recently?

(b) Make a list of the problems facing nuclear families in America.

3 (a) While Christianity and Western morality have done a great deal to reduce polygamy, what adverse social effects has this reduction had on the people of the Kgatla tribe?

(b) What reasons can you suggest for the change in relationship between parents and children?

(c) Give an example from the passage to illustrate the increasing freedom of the young and show the social problems this can bring about.

4 Why do you think that we also use the term nuclear family to apply to the British middle class family? Give at least three reasons to support your answer.

Chapter 7

Roles within the Family

Unit 1: Husbands and Wives

A study of child-rearing practices in pre-industrial societies shows that in the majority of cases it is the boys who are trained in self-reliance, dominance and achievement, and the girls who are trained to take a subservient role. (The Tchambuli of New Guinea are a rare exception to this rule.) Within the societies practising polygamy, the male variation is much more common than the female. Indeed, polyandry usually only occurs as a result of sheer necessity when there are not enough women to go round. The reason for women's secondary status is probably linked to their reproductive function, which makes them in part inefficient workers, but more especially potentially valuable pieces of property. Valuable enough to be bought, sold, swopped, and competed for, but not sufficiently valuable to be thought equal to men in their own right.

With modern influences working on societies, the status of women has altered considerably. The young wife of today is relatively emancipated compared to her Victorian great-grandmother. She is no longer expected to be the mere chattel of her husband, subject to his every whim and deriving her importance solely from his. She now bears him fewer children, and is freed to a great extent from the drudgery of her housework by the spread of modern appliances. She can be educated in the same way, play a complementary part in politics, think in terms of equal pay for equal work, and choose to make a career out of her job rather than out of motherhood.

Emancipation has gone only so far, however, as the Women's Rights Movement is swift to point out. Women's equality in terms of education, employment and power is still an individual rather than a universal achievement, and the majority of women are still content to accept an inferior status.

In Russia, where the majority of doctors and a good third of the engineers are women, social equality is more of a reality. In some countries, however, women are still veiled in Purdah, or offered to guests for the night as a mark of hospitality.

Here are some examples of the roles of husbands and wives in various societies:

D

A. HINDU

Marriage is arranged by relatives and friends, the persons concerned having no choice in the matter. Betrothal frequently takes place at the age of five or six and is regarded as binding. (Marriage follows later.) A man may remarry after being widowed, but custom forbids the woman to do so. Because betrothal takes place so early, and because when a man remarries there is often a great disparity in age between him and his bride, there are many thousands of child widows in India. Although occasionally treated with pity and sympathy, they are regarded as persons of ill-omen, and are often abused until life is made well-nigh intolerable.

A woman's duty to her husband is to bear him sons, who may be profitable in life, and who can offer *pinda* (small balls of rice placed on the ancestral shrine) to him after his death. The law of Manu says 'women were created to be mothers' and the mother is still looked up to by all right-thinking sons. But the lot of a wife may be pitiable if her children are only girls, or if she has none at all. The fact that a dowry must usually be provided when a daughter is married is one very practical reason why parents prefer boys to girls.

One of the most ancient customs in Hindu worship is the provision at all the large temples of groups of *deva-dasis*, or dancing girls, whose duties are those of performing on festival occasions, and of acting as religious prostitutes at other times. Although the giving of small children to be brought up in this way is now illegal, the practice dies hard, and this association of licence with worship is one of the worst features of Hinduism.

Sati, or the act whereby a widow offered herself to be burned alive upon her husband's funeral pyre in order that she might accompany him to the nether world, can be traced back to the earliest times. *Sati* means 'true', and this was once considered the supreme proof of wifely devotion. It was sternly suppressed by the British Government which, however, never interfered with Hindu temple practice.

From 'Hinduism', by Manley and Needing in *The World's Religions*, ed.
Anderson

B. ISLAM

Marriage is expected of every Muslim. The Prophet is reputed to have said, 'Marry women who will love their husbands and be very prolific, for I wish you to be more numerous than any other people'. A Muslim may have as many as, but not more than, four legal wives at any one time; and he may also live with as many slave concubines (mistresses) as he possesses. Besides Muslim women, he may marry Jewesses or Christians and these may continue to practice their own religion, but a Muslim girl may be given in marriage only to another Muslim, and for her there must be no intermarriage of any sort.

When a man has more than one wife he is supposed to divide his time equally between them and to treat them with impartial justice; if he fears he will not be able to do this, he should confine himself to one. A Muslim may divorce his wife at any time and for any reason. It is divorce rather than polygamy – which is decreasingly common – which causes untold suffering to women, and widespread social evils, in Islam today: for it frequently happens that a man will marry a young girl and then, when she has borne him several children and become prematurely aged, divorce her in favour of another adolescent; while the divorced wife can only return to her father and brothers, to be greeted with anything but enthusiasm and married off, if the opportunity occurs, to a second husband, however undesirable. It is not surprising, then, that Muslim women, having no sense of marital security, frequently contrive to put something by against a day of divorce and normally feel more affection for their blood-relatives than their husbands.

In this connection it must be remembered that the seclusion of women in orthodox Islam means that a large number of men marry women that they have never seen and minor children can be compulsorily married off by their fathers.

Women, on their part, can in no circumstances divorce their husbands.

From 'Islam' by Anderson in *The World's Religions*

C. MEXICO

The fathers being indifferent towards their wives and children, spend their money on drink or on mistresses who might even live right there in the same *vecindad* (tenement). If a wife complains, she is likely to be beaten or driven out of the home, because it is her duty to protect her husband from embarrassment in his love affairs. The men spend most of their free time in saloons, and at night the wives might have to hunt them up and half carry them home.

From *Children of Sanchez*, by Oscar Lewis

D. KGATLA TRIBE, SOUTH AFRICA

The wife's inferior status is reflected in the behaviour demanded of her in everyday life. She should pay formal deference to her husband, speaking to him respectfully, waiting upon him, walking before him in the street, and not going about, especially at night, without his knowledge and permission; she sits on the floor, whereas he has his stool or chair; and if strangers come to the compound she must refer them to him and wait in the background while they are talking.

From *Married Life in an African Tribe*, by Isaac Schapera

E. PLAINS INDIANS

The usual response by the Plains Indians of North America to a wife's adultery was to cut off the fleshy part of her nose.

F. MANUS

Among the Manus people of New Guinea, the relationship between husband

and wife is usually strained and cold. Father and mother seem to the child to be two disparate people both playing for him against each other. The blood ties of his parents are stronger than their relationships to each other and there are more factors to pull them apart than there are to draw them together.

From *Growing Up in New Guinea*, by Margaret Mead

G. TCHAMBULI

The Tchambuli women of New Guinea go with shaven heads, unadorned determinedly busy about their affairs. The men wear lovely ornaments, do the shopping, carve and paint and dance. Men whose hair is long enough wear curls, and the others make false curls out of rattan rings. The Tchambuli male is made into an artist by a strong practical woman who spoils and manages him.

From *New Lives for Old*, by Margaret Mead,

H. VICTORIAN ENGLAND

In Victorian England the concept of 'marital unity' meant that the wife had no legal personality independent from that of her husband. This became more sinister for women when they found themselves economically utterly dependent on their husbands. The role of women was conceived to be one of subservience to her husband, the master and ruler of the family. . .

Outside the family, married women had the same legal status as children and lunatics; within it they were their husbands' inferiors. By marriage they moved from dependence on fathers or male relations to dependence on husbands.

From *Captive Wife*, by Hannah Gavron

I. MID-TWENTIETH-CENTURY BRITAIN

(i) 'At the beginning of this century the average woman could expect to spend one third of her life producing children. Today the figure is nearer to one fifteenth.' (Hannah Gavron)

(ii) 'My Dad used to say, "I'm the man of the house. Here's my money. And if anyone wants me, you know where I am – in the pub".'

(iii) 'I don't know how much he earns, I only know what he gives me.'

(iv) 'Men like my father never did much around the house. He found it a strain to pour out a cup of tea. If he saw a man pushing a pram or carrying a kiddy, he'd say he was a cissy. It's all changed now.'

(v) 'Whatever happened in the past, the younger husband of today does not consider that the children belong exclusively to his wife's world, or that he can abandon them to her (and her mother) while he takes his comfort in the male atmosphere of the pub.'

From *Family and Kinship in East London*, by Willmott and Young

J. EMANCIPATION?

'More than a century after Florence Nightingale staged her passionate revolt against the trivial domestic round, here are the mass of women still pre-occupied with their love-life, clothes, children and homes – all the stuff of the women's magazines. . . . The ordinary woman persists in the belief that in marriage, one ounce of perfume is still worth a peck of legal rights and her dreams of power still feature the *femme fatale* rather than the administrative grade of the Civil Service. The working class woman especially is almost untouched by the Women's Movements.'

The 'Economist'

'Few women would want to thumb their noses at husbands, children and community and go off on their own. Those who do may be talented individuals, but they rarely are successful women.'

The 'Redbook'

'In the past 60 years we have come full circle and the American housewife is once again trapped in a squirrel cage. If the cage is now a modern plate-glass-and-broadloom ranch house or a convenient modern apartment, the situation is no less painful than when her grandmother sat over an embroidery hoop in her gilt-and-plush parlour and muttered angrily about women's rights.'

Betty Friedan

Discussion and Written Work

1 Why, in most societies, do women have a status secondary to men?

2 Name one society in which women have a higher status than men.

3 (a) What is the main duty of women in Hindu society?
(b) What is the fate of a barren woman in Hindu society?
(c) Why are boys preferred to girls in Hindu society?
(d) Give an example to illustrate the exploitation of women in Hindu society.

4 Give an example of the way in which Hindu culture perpetuates the subservience of women to men.

5 Which sex has the most status in Islam society? Give at least four clear reasons for your answer.

6 Explain in your own words the status of women in Victorian England.

7 What main changes have taken place in the roles of men and women in Britain during the last 70 years?

8 (a) What is meant by the term 'female emancipation'?
(b) In what important areas have women achieved emancipation in present-day society?
(c) Why are many women still not emancipated in modern industrial societies?
(d) Why are women not emancipated in pre-industrial societies?

Class Project: Men and Women in Society
If you work together in small groups on different aspects of the project, you could, as a class, produce a most interesting piece of work on the status of men and women in society.

SUGGESTED THEMES FOR YOUR PROJECT
1 *Pre-Industrial Societies Compared* – marriage and courtship; men's jobs and women's jobs; cultural traditions and ceremonies.
2 *Victorian England* – relations between husbands and wives in (a) working class families, (b) middle class families; women in factories, mines, and agricultural gangs.
3 *Annie Besant's Birth Control Movement* – beginnings, and gradual acceptance of Family Planning; reasons for the reduction in family size over the last 100 years.
4 *The Suffragettes* – votes for women.
5 *Legal Changes* – divorce; property; care of children; legal aid; abortion.
6 *Working Wives* – expansion of educational opportunity; the 'equal pay issue'; career girls.
7 *The Nuclear Family* – 'home centredness'; increasing partnership in marriage'; importance of women to the consumer market.
8 *Questionnaire to Wives* – do they feel emancipated, inferior, content, bored?
9 *Questionnaire to Husbands* – do they want their wives to work and to earn as much as them? To what extent do they share in the housework and the upbringing of their children?
10 *Sex Indoctrination* – how are children trained to accept the sexual characteristics of their society?
11 *Women in other Advanced Societies* – Russia, America, Sweden, etc.
12 *Women's Liberation* – What is the 'Women's Movement'? In what ways have women not yet achieved equality?
(You can of course add any other relevant themes which interest you, and you should add pictures and photographs to illustrate your investigations.)

Unit 2: The Young

Adolescence

The period in which you are a teenager has been said by many very wise and sympathetic people to be a time of stress and conflict for you. Perhaps you've noticed this, perhaps you haven't. Certainly your experience of adolescence will not be quite like anyone else's, although there are several general experiences which will apply to all of you.

Adolescence is the period in which the young reach physical maturity. Bodily changes make it possible for you to reproduce life and you begin in size and appearance to look more like adults than children.

In pre-industrial societies young people become adults 'almost over-night' and begin to follow with little thought of change or rebellion the pattern of life long practised by their ancestors. In Western industrial societies, however, there is a waiting period between physical maturity and the learning of social maturity before the adolescent is accepted as an adult. Consider these questions together:

(i) When does the law recognise your legal age of majority?

(ii) When do your parents begin to treat you as an adult rather than a child?

(iii) What sort of status – child or adult – do you have at school?

(iv) What sort of status – youngster or adult – would you have in your first job?

Your answers to these questions will indicate that the independence and social acceptance that goes with being an adult is delayed until at least your late teens. During this period there is a great deal to learn, and the more complex a society is the more there is to cause confusion.

Youth Culture

There has grown up in Britain and in many other Western societies an identifiable youth culture centred around music, fashion, leisure activities, attitudes and language, which in this and in its solidarity with other teenagers is distinct from that of any other generation. The main factors which have caused the emergence of an Adolescent Culture in our society are:

(1) *Rapid rate of social change.* This brings to bear many, often conflicting, influences on the child's behaviour adding to the influence of the parents.

(2) *Changing moral and social values.* The more traditional moral code by which parents were brought up is now confronted by the influence of the permissive society.

(3) *The generation conflict.* Here the values and attitudes of the young are often set against those of the old. Role conflicts can occur in an attempt to live up to the expectations of both generations.

(4) *Extended education and the mass media.* Both have made the young better informed than their parents were about the world they live in. They

are more prepared to be critical of things which past generations either did not understand or were willing to accept. Also, staying on at school, and life as a student, provide a situation in which the young are massed together, making it easier for them to form groups and to influence each other.

(5) *Striving for social acceptance.* This is felt to be necessary in a society which encourages competition in schools, in jobs, and in 'being with it'.

(6) *Affluence of the young.* The young have more money to spend on consumer goods, fashions, fads, and entertainments.

(7) *Discovery by Big Business of the lucrative teenage market.* The aim is to get all the money out of the teenagers' pockets.

Discussion and Written Work

1 Write a piece to explain the effect of the following on the typical behaviour of teenagers in this country:
(a) Pop music
(b) Advertising
(c) Dress and appearance
(d) Staying on at school
(e) Earning a living
(f) Votes at 18
(g) The Permissive Society

2 Make a collection of various teenage magazines, then attempt the following:
(a) What types of values, attitudes, behaviour, interests, view of life do they seem to encourage?
(b) What is an 'ideal teenager' like in magazine terms?
(c) In what ways do the magazines' advice to boys and girls differ?
(d) How big a part does advertising and selling play in the magazines' contents?
(e) Estimate what percentage of the magazine is devoted to each of the following items:

fashion	advertising	hobbies and interests
pop music	teenage problems	education
romantic love	world problems	news and current affairs

3 Discuss together the extracts below before attempting the written work:

A. A COMPARISON BETWEEN SAMOAN AND AMERICAN ADOLESCENCE
If it is proved that adolescence is not necessarily a specially difficult period in

a girl's life – and proved it is if we can find any society in which that is so – then what accounts for the presence of storm and stress in American adolescents? First, we may say quite simply that there must be something in the two civilizations to account for the difference. What is there in Samoa which is absent in America, what is there in America which is absent in Samoa, which will account for this difference?

The Samoan background which makes growing up so easy, so simple a matter, is the general casualness of the whole society. For Samoa is a place where no one plays for very high stakes, no one pays very heavy prices, no one suffers for his convictions, or fights to the death for special ends. Disagreements between parent and child are settled by the child's moving across the street, between a man and his village by the man's removal to the next village, between a husband and his wife's seducer by a few fine mats. Neither poverty nor great disasters threaten the people to make them hold their lives dearly and tremble for continued existence. No implacable gods, swift to anger and strong to punish, disturb the even tenor of their days. Wars and cannibalism are long since passed away, and now the greatest cause for tears, short of death itself, is a journey of a relative to another island. No one is hurried along in life or punished harshly for slowness of development. Instead the gifted, the precocious, are held back, until the slowest among them have caught the pace. And in personal relations, caring is as slight. Love and hate, jealousy and revenge, sorrow and bereavement, are all matters of weeks. From the first months of its life, when the child is handed carelessly from one woman's hands to another's, the lesson is learned of not caring for one person greatly, not setting high hopes on any one relationship.

In this casual attitude towards life, in this avoidance of conflict, of poignant situations, Samoa contrasts strongly not only with America but also with most primitive civilizations. And however much we may deplore such an attitude and feel that important personalities and great art are not born in so shallow a society, we much recognize that here is a strong factor in the painless development from childhood to womanhood. For where no one feels very strongly, the adolescent will not be tortured by poignant situations. There are no such disastrous choices as those which confronted young people who felt that the service of God demanded forswearing the world for ever, as in the Middle Ages, or cutting off one's finger as a religious offering, as among the Plains Indians. So, high up in our list of explanations we must place the lack of deep feeling which the Samoans have conventionalized until it is the very framework of all their attitudes towards life.

And next there is the most striking way in which all isolated primitive civilizations and many modern ones differ from our own, in the number of choices which are permitted to each individual. Our children grow up to find a world of choices dazzling their unaccustomed eyes. In religion they may be

Catholics, Protestants, Christian Scientists, Spiritualists, Agnostics, Atheists, or even pay no attention at all to religion. This is an unthinkable situation in any primitive society not exposed to foreign influence. There is one set of gods, one accepted religious practice.

The close relationship between parent and child, which has such a decisive influence upon so many in our civilization that submission to the parent or defiance of the parent may become the dominating pattern of a lifetime, is not found in Samoa. Children reared in households where there are half a dozen adult women to care for them and dry their tears, and a half dozen adult males, all of whom represent constituted authority, do not distinguish their parents as sharply as our children do.

The lack of specialized feeling which results from this diffusion of affection in the household is further reinforced by the segregation of the boys from the girls, so that a child regards the children of the opposite sex as taboo relatives, regardless of individuality, or as present enemies and future lovers, again regardless of individuality.

By the time she reaches puberty the Samoan girl has learned to subordinate choice in the selection of friends or lovers to an observance of certain categories. Friends must be relatives of one's own sex; lovers, non-relatives.

Nothing could present a sharper contrast to the average American home, with its small number of children, the close, theoretically permanent tie between the parents, the drama of the entrance of each new child upon the scene and the deposition of the last baby. Here the growing girl learns to depend upon a few individuals, to expect the rewards of life from certain kinds of personalities. With this first set towards preference in personal relations she grows up playing with boys as well as with girls, learning to know well brothers and cousins and schoolmates. She does not think of boys as a class but as individuals, nice ones like the brother of whom she is fond, or disagreeable, domineering ones, like a brother with whom she is always on bad terms. Preference in physical make-up, in temperament, in character, develops and forms the foundations for a very different adult attitude in which choice plays a vivid role. The Samoan girl never tastes the rewards of romantic love as we know it, nor does she suffer as an old maid who has appealed to no lover or found no lover appealing to her, or as the frustrated wife in a marriage which has not fulfilled her high demands.

From *Coming of Age in Samoa*, by Margaret Mead

1 'Life in Samoa is very casual'. Give as many examples from the passage as you can to illustrate this remark.
2 What effect does this casualness of life have on the period of adolescence?
3 Give two examples of ways in which the American adolescent has to choose between differing sorts of behaviour, while the Samoan adolescent has only one pattern of behaviour to accept.

4 What factors in the early social experience of Samoan children have prevented them from becoming neurotic?

5 How much choice has the Samoan girl in picking friends and boy-friends?

6 An American girl usually experiences much closer family ties and can choose a future husband for herself. Why do these two facts sometimes produce emotional problems for the American girl?

B. THE GENERATION GAP

(Camara Laye is a young Negro from French West Africa. At 15 he left his home in the village of Kouroussa to go to the technical college on the coast 400 miles away. At the end of each year he returns home for the holidays.)

Each time I went back home to spend my holidays at Kouroussa I would find my hut newly decorated with white clay; my mother would be all impatience to show me the improvements which she had made in it from year to year.

'Well, what do you think of it?' my mother would say.

'It's wonderful,' I would reply.

And I would give her a great hug: that was all the thanks my mother expected. But it was indeed 'wonderful' and I did not suspect how much ingenuity had gone into it.

The main article of furniture, the one which immediately caught the eye, was the divan bed. At first, it had just been like the one in her own hut, a bed like any other bed in our country, a bed made of clay bricks. Then the central bricks had been removed, leaving only two supports, one at the foot and one at the head; and planks had taken the place of the bricks. On this improvised bedstead – crude but not uncomfortable – my mother finally placed a mattress stuffed with rice straw. Thus it became a comfortable and fairly spacious bed, big enough for three or even four.

But it was hardly spacious enough to accommodate all the friends, the innumerable friends, both boys and girls, who would come and visit me on certain evenings. I cannot remember just how, piled all together on the bed, we managed to find room to strum a guitar, nor yet how my friends got enough air for singing.

I do not know whether my mother cared very much for these meetings but she put up with them, comforting herself probably with the thought that at least I was in my own compound, not hanging around Lord knows where. As for my father, he thought it was quite in order. As I scarcely saw him at all during the day, busy as I was visiting this or that friend's house (if I had not gone off on some more expensive trip), he would come and knock on my door. I would cry: 'Come in' and he would enter, saying good evening to everyone, and would ask me how I had spent my day. After a few more words, he would go away. He understood that, although his presence was welcome – and it really was – it was at the same time very intimidating to such a lively and youthful gathering as ours.

My mother's attitude was completely different. Her hut was close to mine and their doors faced each other: my mother had only to take a single step, and she was inside my hut. She used to do so without any warning; she never knocked at the door, she just walked straight in. Suddenly, there she would be, standing before us, without the slightest sound from the door; she would look closely at everyone before saying good evening.

Oh! it was not the faces of my men friends that she scrutinized; they were my own affair; they did not matter. No, it was the girls' faces that my mother used to inspect; and she very soon picked out the faces she did not like. I must admit that in these gatherings there were sometimes young women of rather loose habits, and whose reputation was a little tarnished. But how could I forbid them to come? Did I even want to do so? If they were a little more worldly wise than was necessary, they were also generally the most amusing. But my mother thought otherwise, and she never used to beat about the bush.

'You,' she would say, 'what are you doing here? Your place is not with my son. Go back home. If I see you here again, I'll have something to tell your mother about you. I warn you.'

If the girl did not make off fast enough, or if she did not extract herself quickly enough from the jumble on the divan, my mother would pull her out by the arm and thrust her towards the open door.

'Go on,' she would cry, 'get back home.'

And with her hands she would pretend to be chasing away some too adventurous fowl. Only then would she say good evening to everyone.

I did not care much for this procedure, I did not care for it at all. Reports of these insults were spread abroad; and whenever I invited a girlfriend to come and visit me, she would say as often as not:

'And what if your mother catches me?'

'She won't eat you.'

'No but she'll start shouting and show me the door.'

And I would stand there in front of the girl, wondering: 'Is there any reason why my mother should turn her out of doors?' And I did not always know. I used to live in Conakry for the greater part of the year, and I did not know all the details of Kouroussa gossip. But I could hardly say to the girl: 'Have people been talking about you? And if you've had any affairs, do you think my mother knows about them?' It exasperated me.

As I grew older I became more passionate; I no longer had merely half-hearted friendships – or even love affairs. I did not only have Marie or Fanta – although at first it was Marie and Fanta I had as friends. But Marie was on holiday at Bela, at her father's; and Fanta was my 'regular' girl. I respected her; and even if I had wanted to go further (and I did not want to) custom would have forbidden it. The rest . . . the rest were unimportant, but they existed nevertheless. Could my mother fail to understand the growing ardour of my blood?

She understood it only too well. Often she would get up in the middle of the night and come and make sure that I was alone in bed. She would generally make her rounds towards midnight, striking a match to light my bed. If I still happened to be awake, I would pretend to be asleep; then as if the lighted match had disturbed me I would pretend to wake with a start.

'What's the matter?' I would cry.

'Are you asleep?' my mother would ask.

'Yes, I was asleep. Why did you wake me?'

'Good, go to sleep again.'

'But how can I sleep if you keep waking me up?'

'Don't get worked up,' she would cry. 'Go to sleep.'

But I did not care much for this kind of treatment. And I used to complain about it to Kouyate and Check Omar, who were at that time my most intimate friends.

'Am I not old enough to look after myself?' I would ask. 'I was considered sufficiently grown up to be given my own hut; but how can I call my hut my own if people can enter it at any hour of the day or night?'

'It shows that your mother loves you very much,' they would answer. 'You are not going to complain of that?'

'No,' was all I could say.

From *The African Child*, by Camara Laye

1 Give three examples from the passage to describe the living conditions in the village of Kouroussa.

2 In what way did the father show understanding of the feelings of young people?

3 In what three ways did the mother's behaviour embarrass her son?

4 Why was the boy annoyed by his mother's behaviour, do you think?

5 Explain from your own experience and reading some of the conflicts that can arise between adolescents and their parents.

(a) How do their attitudes and values differ from each other?

(b) In each case explain:

    (i) the parents' point of view

    (ii) the point of view of the adolescents

C. SANDRA

(In many of the older areas of cities there are no recreational facilities for young people and many can soon find themselves in trouble with the police.)

Besides roaming round the streets (the boys generally in gangs, the girls in smaller, less cohesive groups), a piece of waste land near the docks is a favourite playground. Old pots and pans and other metal objects extracted from a near-by scrapyard help to furnish the site as an ideal place for wonderful, if occasionally dangerous games of the imagination. A café (later closed by the police) attracts many of the younger boys during the earlier hours of the evening (i.e. five to nine thirty). On one occasion I saw them running wild in here, puffing at stumps of cigarettes with great seriousness, dashing from one side of the room to the other and fighting. Their strength and energy were almost terrifying. Needless to say, most are already in trouble with the police . . . Many of their families are notorious for their delinquency. In such families there is a shortage of room and a lack of interest at home. This seems to mean that, out of school, their time and activities are entirely unsupervised. An adventure playground might be interesting.

Sandra is one who has this unchained and brute freedom to excess. There are no restrictions on the time she should be home at night, meals are rarely cooked affairs, and times are very erratic. Invariably when I ask her if it is not time she went home (because it is late/dark/dinner-time her mother will wonder where she has been for the past four/six hours) she replies that her 'mother won't mind'. This appears to be the truth. I knew the mother quite well, a friendly but hopeless woman, thin, pale, and tired-looking, who seems to have given up trying to impose her will on anyone. The family is large; the father works erratically and drinks heavily . . .

Sandra wanders around Lymport, Avonmore, and sometimes to Northtown often alone or sometimes with a friend. Friendships with children of her own age seem to last only a short time, but she has brought an odd assortment to the flat including an educationally sub-normal boy who throws bricks through windows whenever annoyed . . . It seems quite certain that she is delinquent and has been for some time. She was recently caught shop-lifting but the case was not taken to court . . .

From *The Unattached*, by Mary Morse

1 How do the young people in this area spend their leisure time?
2 What sort of families do these children come from and how does this affect their behaviour?
3 Explain why Sandra's family does not provide the order and security she needs for her good behaviour.
4 Why do you think Sandra is 'often alone' or with friends who 'last only a short time'?

5 Given the fact that problem families exist in an area like this, make three suggestions of ways in which the authorities could help these children.

D. BLACK BOY

Night would fall. Bats would zip through the air. Crickets would cry from the grass. Frogs would croak. The stars would come out. Dew would dampen the earth. Yellow squares of light would glow in the distance as kerosene lamps were lit in our homes. Finally, from across the fields or down the road a long slow yell would come:

'Youuuuuuu Daaaaaavee!'

Easy laughter among the boys but no reply.

'Calling the hogs.'

'Go home, pig.'

Laughter again. A boy would slowly detach himself from the gang.

'Youuuuuuu Daaaaaavee!'

He would not answer his mother's call, for that would have been a sign of dependence. The boy would trot home slowly and there would be more easy laughter. More talk. One by one we would be called home to fetch water from the hydrant in the back yard, to go to the store and buy greens and meal for tomorrow, to split wood for kindling.

We were now large enough for the white boys to fear us and both of us, the white boys and black boys, began to play our traditional racial roles as though we had been born to them, as though it was in our blood, as though we were being guided by instinct. All the frightful descriptions we had heard about each other, all the violent expressions of hate and hostility that had seeped into us from our surroundings, came now to the surface to guide our actions. The roundhouse was the racial boundary of the neighbourhood, and it had been tacitly agreed between the white boys and the black boys that the whites were to keep to the far side of the roundhouse and we blacks were to keep to our side. Whenever we caught a white boy on our side we stoned him: if we strayed to their side they stoned us.

Our battles were real and bloody; we threw rocks, cinders, coal, sticks, pieces of iron, and broken bottles, and while we threw them we longed for even deadlier weapons. If we were hurt, we took it quietly; there was no crying or whimpering. If our wounds were not truly serious, we hid them from our parents. We did not want to be beaten for fighting. Once, in a battle with a gang of white boys, I was struck behind the ear with a piece of broken bottle; the cut was deep and bled profusely. I tried to stem the flow of blood by dabbing at the cut with a rag and when my mother came from work I was forced to tell her that I was hurt, for I needed medical attention. She rushed me to a Doctor, who stitched my scalp; but when she took me home she beat me, telling me that I must never fight white boys again, that I might be killed by them, that she had to work and had no time to worry about my fights. Her words did not sink in, for they conflicted with the code of the streets. I promised my mother that I would not fight, but I knew that if I kept my word I would lose my standing in the gang, and the gang's life was my life.

From *Black Boy*, by Richard Wright

1 Explain the gang's attitudes to:
(a) mothering
(b) colour prejudice
(c) the casualties of war
(d) gang loyalty
2 In what ways did the mother's attitude to fighting white boys differ from her sons?

Unit 3: The Elderly

Pre-Industrial Societies

In pre-industrial societies, the oldest people of the community are usually treated with great respect. In a society where there are no books, written records, or mass-media, the old, with the longest memories, preserve the link with the past, and with the customs, traditions, and beliefs of former times. The old frequently control the extended family group and as such have great authority in the society. They are in many cases closely linked with the religious beliefs of the group and this also increases their status. In societies which believe in life after death, the elderly deceased are made into family gods and are worshipped by the living through the mediation of the eldest living relative.

Ancestor Worship

The Kgatla believed in the survival of the dead. It was held that the souls of dead people became spirits, which ultimately found their way to a world vaguely located somewhere underground. Here they led a life very similar to that on earth. But they continued also to take an active interest in the fortunes of their living descendants, over whose behaviour they exercised a powerful control. They rewarded with good health and prosperity those who treated them with becoming respect and obedience, but punished with sickness, economic loss, or other misfortune those who neglected them or who offended against the prevailing social code, of which they were the guardians. In order, therefore, to retain their favour, no opportunity was lost of attempting to please them. The worship of the dead was in fact the outstanding feature of Kgatla religion.

Each family was held to be under the direct guidance of its own ancestors, who in turn were interested only in the affairs of their own descendants. They retained the individual characteristics they had possessed while alive, and their importance as deities was determined largely by the status they had enjoyed on earth. In practice worship was generally directed only to those more recently dead, like a father or grandfather, whose personal peculiarities were known and remembered. The head of the family, as senior living representative of the ancestors, conducted the rites. He sacrificed and prayed to the dead whenever they revealed themselves through dreams or calamity or in some other form that the diviners interpreted as a sign that they were offended. He also invoked them on all important domestic occasions, like birth, marriage, or the undertaking of some new enterprise, when he offered them libations of beer or sacrifices of fowls, goats, and in emergencies even cattle, and prayed to them for continued guidance and help, or thanked them for the blessings they had sent. His role of family priest gave him considerable authority over his dependants; they could not approach their ancestors except through his agency, so that if they quarrelled with him they were cut off from the deities controlling their welfare. A special ceremony of reconciliation was then necessary before he would again sacrifice on their behalf.

From *Married Life in an African Tribe*, by Isaac Schapera

Industrial Societies

In our society, the elderly have a very different status from the highly respected leadership function they assume in many pre-industrial communities. In the West, the emphasis is rather on youth, and the most influential people in the community are probably those who are at the height of their career in their early middle age. In the pace of modern living the old seem increasingly to be left behind, and while at best they can become doting grandparents, loved and cared for by their family, at worst they can often find themselves ailing, lonely, and without much use.

In the movement to the nuclear family there is frequently no place for the old, and the responsibility for their welfare has been substantially taken over by the state, through, for example, pension schemes, social security, community day centres, and old people's homes. As the proportion of elderly people in our society increases because of the reduction of fatal illnesses, a higher standard of living and longer life expectancy, the problems of old age become more apparent and more pressing.

The Problems of Old Age

The self-esteem and status of old people suffer today partly because our present values – stressed by advertising and the mass media – are focused to a large extent on youth. The old are therefore more likely to feel that they lack security, that they do not belong, and that they cannot make any worthwhile contribution to society.

New social and economic developments mean that young people are less likely to settle near their parents in the home area. As a result, the elderly may be left without family contacts or anyone to care for them in sickness. These unsupported and isolated people place the greatest burden on medical and welfare services. The published figures show that single, widowed and divorced people make much more demand on hospital accommodation than those who live in a marriage partnership. This situation has been made worse by the development of new housing areas, which tend to be occupied mainly by younger people with children.

Breaking family ties in this way not only tends to isolate old people, but deprives the younger generations of relationships which are valuable to them. Long distances and transport costs make it difficult to preserve the frequent contact which is needed to keep affection and mutual support alive between the generations. A family which includes members of three (or even more) generations is best for the mental health of all concerned, for old people can help in bringing up young children, and by taking an active part in family life can give a young married couple free time together which they would not otherwise have.

Retirement from work is particularly disturbing, for social status and personal interests are closely involved in work, especially for men. The problem becomes more serious as fixed retiring ages grow more common. Our society as at present ordered does not use as fully as it might the abilities and experience of the old.

Retirement also usually involves a reduced income. The great advances in state benefits and in pensions attached to employment cushion but do not eliminate this shock, and they are partly offset not only by inflation but by the rising standards of living which make old people expect more than mere subsistence. Many ill effects follow from lack of money; not only physical hardship, such as cold or malnutrition, but restriction of customary activities and social contacts.

Public authorities pressed to house young married people with families cannot allot a large part of their resources to building dwellings suitable for the elderly. Failure to find a suitable place to live accentuates every other trouble of old age and adds to the sense of living in a society which has no place for the old.

From 'The Problems of Old Age' – Pamphlet 4, Mental Health Trust and Research Fund

Discussion and Written Work

1 (a) Why does ancestor worship ensure that the elderly in the Kgatla tribe are held in great esteem by the younger people?

(b) Why was the senior living representative of the ancestors particularly powerful in the family?

(c) In what important ways was the influence of the past and of the recently dead preserved in community activities?

(d) What effects do you think these have had on the status of the elderly in Kgatla Society:
(i) Christianity?
(ii) Modernisation?

2 (a) Why are the elderly likely to feel out of place in our own society today?

(b) What social movements have caused the increasing isolation of old people?

(c) How could closer family relationships improve 'the mental health of all concerned'?

(d) What effects does retirement have on an individual's:
(i) Social status?
(ii) Standard of living?
(iii) Social relationships?

(e) What type of houses are most suitable for elderly people? Why are there not enough of these to go round?

115

3 MISS PALEY

Miss Paley, aged sixty-seven, lived in a one-room tenement flat. It was a large airless room with dismal orange-brown wallpaper peeling off in huge strips. Two or three mats, ingrained with dirt, covered the floor. There was an old iron bedstead propped up in the middle by two strips of wood and on this was a heap of grey and brown blankets. An ancient iron mangle stood in a corner and there was a gas stove, a gas mantle for lighting, three or four wooden chairs, and a table with a flat-iron propping up one of its legs. Miss Paley wore a pair of stockings, extensively patched and tied around her knees, and a ramshackle navy-blue skirt and slip. Her skin had the whiteness of someone who rarely went out and she was very shy of her appearance, particularly the open sores on her face. She said she suffered from blood poisoning, but had not seen her doctor since the war. (This was confirmed by the doctor.) She was the only child of parents who had been street traders and who had died when she was young, in the 1880s. 'I was with my aunt until I was nearly forty. She was eighty-five when she died. I had cousins in the street but they were my aunt's children. In the war they got scattered. They all had families to bring up and I haven't met them since the war. I don't know where they are. They had to leave me behind. I don't want them people. I do my work in my own way. They wouldn't have the patience with me.' Persistent questioning failed to reveal a single relative with whom she had any contact. She did not go to the cinema, to a club, or to church, and had no radio. She spent Christmas on her own and had never had a holiday away from home. She sometimes made conversation with her neighbours in the street but because of her appearance did not go into their homes or they into hers. She had only one friend, a young woman who 'used to live in the street where I lived', and they visited one another about once a week. Her answer to a question about membership of a club was typical of much she said. 'No, I can't be shut in. I don't go to those clubs. They'd be too much excitement for me.' At one point she said she went to bed about 8 p.m. and got up between 10 and 11 the next day. I also found she had an hour or two in bed in the afternoons.

From *The Family Life of Old People*, by Peter Townsend

(a) What evidence is there in this character study that Miss Paley was:
  (i) very poor?
  (ii) very lonely?
(b) Do you know any old people who are like Miss Paley? What can the state and voluntary organisations do to help people like this?

Survey of the Elderly in East Hull

The purpose of a survey, conducted jointly by the College of Education and David Lister School in Hull during the first two weeks of July, 1970, was to find the number of old people living in the vicinity of the school and the addresses where they lived. A sample of these was then interviewed to find out about their way of life and their social needs. The school already did much to help the elderly in its area, and the information from the survey was to enable this work to be extended, either by the school itself or by other agencies.

CENSUS

College student and school sixth-former worked together in pairs and located initially the places of residence of all persons aged 60 and over who live adjacent to the school; the area covered was bounded by Holderness Road and Southcoates Lane and was equivalent to one ward in the city. The Register of Electors gave 7,270 adults aged 18 and over as living in the area, and the census located 1,350 elderly, which was almost 20% of the adult population.

SAMPLE

A sample of the elderly was chosen by taking every sixth name from the census list giving a sample size of 226. These were then interviewed by a student and sixth-former together. The response rate was rather disappointing: 163 interviews took place, which was 72% of the sample size. Much of the non-response was due to the elderly person not wanting to be interviewed, some was the result of absence in hospital, etc., and some interviews could not be completed because the interviewee was too ill or senile to answer the questions. However, apart from the sex balance, the people interviewed appeared to be representative of the population, as the following shows:

Age and Married Status	Sample of 163	1966 National Census: Hull
% Aged 60–69	56.4	57.6
% Aged 75 and over	24.5	24.1
% Married of all 60 +	57.1	54.5
% Single of all 60 +	9.2	9.6
% Female of all 60 +	66.9	60

The sample had an over-representation of females, which could be the result of women being more likely to be at home when the interviewers called during the day.

MAIN FINDINGS FROM THE SAMPLE ENQUIRY

This area in Hull is predominantly working class. Only 9.2% of the sample were salary-earner status or equivalent; 89% were wage-earner status; 3 people were not able to be classified. Nearly all the sample left school when they were 14 or less; 94% came within this category, leaving 6% who stayed at school until they were 15 or older.

HOUSEHOLD ARRANGEMENTS

A large number of the elderly lived alone or just with a husband or wife. Not a large proportion lived with a daughter or son; only about 24 out of the 163 (15%) interviewed lived in this kind of household. The following gives the two main types of household arrangement:

Persons aged 60+ living alone or with spouse

	Number	Percentage
Living alone	51	31%
Living with spouse only	69	42%
Other household arrangement	43	27%
Total	163	100%

This shows that nearly ¾ (73%) lived alone or just with a spouse. When those aged 70 and over were considered separately, the preponderance of this type of household is even greater: 47% lived alone and 31% lived just with a spouse (over ¾ (78%) of this age group). Thus for the older people in the sample, the commonest arrangement was a single person household and this seemed to increase with age. There were 18 people in the sample who were aged 80 or over, and of these 12 or ⅔ lived alone.

HOUSEHOLD AMENITIES AND HOME ENTERTAINMENT

Basic Household Amenities

% of dwellings with:	1966 National Census: Hull	Sample
No inside lavatory	33%	36%
No fixed bath	26%	44%
No hot tap in dwelling	21%	52%

In 1966, ⅓ of the dwellings in Hull had no indoor lavatory, ¼ had no fixed bath and 1 in 5 had no hot tap in them. According to the sample, the elderly in this part of Hull are without an indoor lavatory in over ⅓ of their dwellings and in over ½ of old people's homes there was no hot tap – a very large proportion compared with the rest of the city. In marked contrast, the elderly in the sample fared well for entertainment at home: the vast majority had T.V. and radio and took newspapers. 87% had a T.V. set and over 90% had a radio; only 17 people said they did not get a newspaper every day, and only 2 people in the sample never received a daily newspaper.

GOING OUT

The elderly were asked how they had spent the previous 7 days. Sixteen (10%) had not been out of their house during the previous week. The remaining 90% had been out of the house at least once that week. The typical outing was to go to the shop, or for a walk, or to make a call on a relative or friend. Other types of outing were made by only a minority of the elderly; 38 had attended a club, 15 had been to church, and 12 had been to bingo.

CONTACT WITH RELATIVES

Old people in this part of Hull saw a lot of their relatives, and they feature in their lives a great deal. If an old person who lives alone does not belong to a club or go to church, and does not see much of neighbours, then relatives can be his only regular social contacts. They were asked how many of their relatives they had seen in the 7 days prior to the survey ('seen' included contact by letter or telephone) and whether or not it had been a typical week for contact.

Taking the 70+ age group, of which half lived alone, the average number of relatives seen was just over 4 (4.2%).

HELP FROM WELFARE AND OTHER ORGANISATIONS

Sixty-two of the sample belonged to some club or society, and for 15 of these it was the Old People's Club run by the School. However, when the old people were asked if they had ever had any help in their homes from such as health visitors, Meals-on-Wheels, welfare workers, or from vicar or minister, 123 or 76% said no such help had ever been given. Sixty-six per cent of the sample said they thought that not enough was done to help the elderly these days, and when they were asked whose responsibility they thought it was to care for them, only 18% said they thought it should be their relatives: 62% expressed the opinion that the state should take responsibility.

CONCLUSIONS

There is obviously much that could be done to cater for the social and other needs of the elderly in East Hull. The majority of the sample (62%)

did not belong to a club or society, but the unsatisfied need for this kind of social life may not be great as only 49 of the 163 said they enjoyed old people's gatherings usually, and 47 said they did *not* enjoy them.

What would seem to require attention, however, was indicated by the fact that the large majority had never had any assistance from those agencies which exist to help the elderly. Perhaps the greatest need in an area like this is for organised visits to the homes of the elderly and advice given on where and how they can get help when it is required. Visiting old people, armed with basic knowledge of the state and voluntary services that are available so that they can be informed of the facilities provided for them in the community, would, the researchers concluded, be a valuable service for the elderly.

Discussion and Written Work

1 (a) What was the purpose of the survey?
(b) Explain carefully:
(i) What is meant by a sample.
(ii) How the sample of elderly people was drawn up.
(iii) Why the sample response rate was rather disappointing.
(c) Explain *in your own words* the difference between people of 'salary-earner status' and people of 'wage-earner status'.
(d) (i) What seems to be the normal pattern of household arrangements for the elderly in this area? Give statistical evidence from the survey to support your answer.
(ii) Suggest reasons for this type of household arrangements.
(e) (i) How did the basic household amenities of the sample compare with those of Hull as a whole?
(ii) What does this tell you about the kind of area investigated?
(f) How do the elderly in the area spend their leisure time?
(g) Give some examples from your own knowledge or experience to show how relatives feature a great deal in the lives of the elderly in an area like this.
(h) What percentage of the elderly had been offered help in their homes by the state or voluntary organisations?
(i) What recommendations does the survey make in the light of its findings?

2 CLASS PROJECT ON ELDERLY PEOPLE IN YOUR DISTRICT
How does the life of elderly people in your area compare with the findings of this survey? The only way to find out accurately would be to conduct a survey of your own. Discuss the size of your sample with your teacher. How will you draw it up? How many people will you interview?

Here is a questionnaire to help you. Think of other questions of your own which you would like to add.

(Explain to each person interviewed on first meeting: 'We are from .... school and we are conducting a survey about elderly people in this area. We want to obtain some general facts about older people as part of our studies and should like to ask you some questions about your way of life. If it is not convenient to talk now could we call again in the next few days?')

Sex of Respondent	M ( ) F ( )
1. First could we ask you your opinion about whether you think enough is done to help the elderly these days?	Yes ( ) No ( ) D.K. ( )
2. Could you tell us if you live alone, or if anyone else lives with you?	Parent ( ) Grandchild ( ) Spouse ( ) Great-grandchild ( ) Sibling ( ) Child ( ) In-law ( ) Lodger ( )
(Tick or number in brackets)	Other ....
3. Could we now ask you about your home: Have you any of the following in your house?	Radio ( ) T.V. ( ) Telephone ( ) Indoor lavatory ( ) Bath which is fixed ( ) Hot water ( )
4. Do you get a newspaper?	Every week-day ( ) Sunday ( ) Sometimes ( ) Never ( )
5. Have you ever had any help from any of the following? Have they helped you at all this year?	Meals-on-wheels ( ) This year ( ) Home help, This year ( ) Health visitor or Home nurse ( ) This year ( ) Welfare worker ( ) This year ( ) Vicar, Minister ( ) This year ( ) Youth Action Young person ( ) This year ( )
6. How long have you lived in this home?	Over 30 years ( ) Between 11 and 30 years ( ) Between 6 and 10 years ( ) Five years or less ( )

7. (*If less than 11 years in this home*)
   Where did you move from when you   This neighbourhood ( )
   came here?   Elsewhere in the city ( )
      Outside the city ( )

8. Can we ask your opinion about   State ( )
   whether the state or relatives should   Relatives ( )
   mainly care for the elderly?   D. K. ( )

9. Could you now tell us something   (specify subjects) ....
   about your school days?   ....
       (a) What subjects do you remember   ....
          doing?   ....

       (b) Do you remember going on any   Yes ( )   No ( )
          visits organised by the school?
          If Yes: What kind, for instance?   ....

       (c) What kinds of punishment did
          the teachers use?   ....

       (d) Were there some poor children   No coat: Some ( ) Many ( )
          who came to school in winter   No-one ( )
          without a coat, or had no shoes?   No shoes: Some ( ) Many ( )
                 No-one ( )

       (e) Do you remember the school   Yes ( )   No ( )
          doing anything to find them
          clothes/shoes?
          If Yes: What did the school   ....
          do?   ....

       (f) What age were you when you   15 + ( ) 14 ( ) 13 ( )
          left school?   12 or less ( )

10. Finally, would you mind telling us
    your age, whether married or not,
    and your occupation?
        (a) Which age group do you belong   60–64 ( ) 65–69 ( ) 70–74 ( )
           to?   75–79 ( ) 80–84 ( )
              85 or over ( )

        (b) Are you, or have you been,   Married ( )   Single ( )
           married?   Widowed ( )   Divorced or
                  Separated ( )

        (c) *If man*: What was your occupa-   (Occupation):
           tion just before you retired or   ....
           what is it now?   ....
           If married woman: What is, or   ....
           was, your husband's occupa-   ....
           tion?   ....

If single woman: What was your   ....

occupation?   ....

If widowed/div./sep.: What was   ....

your former husband's occupa-   ....

tion?   ....

Thank you for letting us interview you and for your co-operation.

Interviewer's name ....

Date of Interview   ....

3 INTERPRETING YOUR FINDINGS

When you have completed all the interviews and collected all the information together, you can best interpret your findings by answering the following questions:

(a) (i) What percentage felt that not enough was being done for the elderly today?

(ii) Did the majority feel that relatives or the state should be responsible for the care of the elderly?

(b) What percentage of the elderly in your sample:

(i) lived alone?

(ii) lived with spouse?

(iii) lived with relatives?

(c) What percentage lived in houses which lacked basic amenities?

(d) Give statistical evidence to show how much help the old people got from welfare and voluntary organisations.

(e) How long had they been living in their present homes?

(f) From the information the old people gave about their schooldays, write a piece to compare their school experience with your own.

(g) What percentage of the elderly in your sample were:

(i) married?

(ii) single?

(iii) widowed?

(iv) divorced or separated?

(h) From the information given about their occupations and the type of housing they were in, say what percentage of the sample were working class and what percentage were middle class.

4 Now look again at the results of the survey carried out in East Hull to assess how your findings compare with the findings of the East Hull survey. Then write a careful and detailed report to compare the two pieces of research.

Chapter 8

Socialisation

Strange as it may seem, infants have first of all to learn to behave in a human way, and then to learn the culture – the whole way of life – of their society.

They are born with a certain amount of innate ability and various personal qualities, which differ from child to child and which considerably affect the child's later development in life. They are also born with a vast amount of potential for learning, which is common to all children. The way in which this potential is used depends upon the life experiences of the child. In this sense, his social environment is vitally important, because it is from this environment that, using his own powers, he learns the language, behaviour, customs, attitudes, and mannerisms of its particular culture. A child brought up in the igloo of an Eskimo family in Alaska will learn a totally different culture from the child raised in a floating reed hut of the Marsh Arabs in Iraq. Similarly, a child who learns the middle class sub-culture of a well-to-do suburban family in Kent or Essex will have had a very different life experience from the child brought up in a coal-miner's family in the Welsh Valleys, or in a small fishing community in the Outer Hebrides. The different environments of these children will have played an enormous part in moulding the potential they all share for learning, and in affecting the ways in which they have learned to behave.

The Nature-Nurture Controversy
In the past sociologists were unable to agree which factor in the infant's make-up was most important in his later development. There were those who argued that his nature, his innate ability, the biological characteristics which he inherited and was born with, were of absolute importance in deciding his future life; and there were those who replied that the environment which nurtured him, the experiences he learned in his daily life, were the most important factors in deciding what type of person he would be. This argument came to be known as the Nature-Nurture Controversy and there were many supporters of both sides. Today, however, we have come to realise that it is a combination of the two factors working together which produces the man; neither his innate ability nor the influence of his environment can be separated from the other. What has long been neglected,

however, is an understanding of just how influential a factor the environment is and how inadequate are the purely biological mechanisms of a child when they act in isolation (see 'Anna' and 'Isabelle', pp. 128–130)

Animal Studies

In an effort to test the effects of socialisation, it has rarely been possible to use actual children for experiments since this could prove cruel or harmful. Experiments have been carried out on animals, however, particularly apes, chimps, and monkeys, which are the nearest species to man in the animal kingdom.

Humans can do very few things when they are born and are dependent upon their mothers for a long period until their bodies and senses develop, and until they learn patterns of human behaviour. Animals are born with instinctive behaviour, however, and can look after themselves almost immediately without being taught. Only in primates (apes, chimps and monkeys) is there a learning process which in any way resembles that of humans.

Discussion and Written Work

Discuss the following studies of animals and children, then attempt the written work:

1 *Testing the Instinctive Behaviour of Otters and Baboons*

Both baboon and otter were taken away from their mothers shortly after birth. The baboon was reared under our own supervision by a human foster-mother. The baby otter, whose captured mother died from wounds immediately after its birth, was placed among a litter of puppies and accepted by the bitch. Both were carefully kept from all contact with their own kind and all knowledge of their natural environment.

The otter was reared thirty miles from the running stream. The only water supply in the vicinity was a deep well, and it never, at any one time, saw more water than was necessary to quench its thirst. It never saw a fish or crab and was fed exclusively on raw meat. When fully grown, it was taken for the first time to a river pool. It ran down to the water, smelled it and drank some. Then it struck the surface two or three times with its paw and immediately plunged in, diving, swimming and 'playing' just as a wild otter does. It had not been fed for some considerable time, and within half an hour it had captured a small fish and then a crab.

Our artificially reared baboon came from a district where its natural food supply would have consisted almost exclusively of insects and wild fruits. The wild baboon obtains insects by turning over all the big stones in its line of march and is especially fond of the very abundant scorpions. This is a delicacy relished by wild baboons throughout South Africa and they show great ingenuity in catching them. The scorpion is rapidly beaten about with the hand until half-dazed, and is then turned on its back by a flick of the fingers and seized by the legs. In this position it cannot sting. The tail containing the sting and poison sac is carefully removed before eating. I have never seen a wild baboon stung by a scorpion during this process. Among the wild fruit commonly eaten there are several tempting-looking drupes and berries which are poisonous. I have never seen a wild baboon meddle with a poison plant or attempt to pick a poison fruit. They carefully avoid them. Quite small youngsters seem to know the danger.

To this, its natural environment, our captive baboon was suddenly introduced for the first time when it was nearly full grown. It had been deprived of food for long enough to make it extremely hungry, but although it was in the midst of unturned stones covering innumerable insects, it had no idea of turning them over, nor could direct suggestion awake any hereditary memory. When a stone was turned exposing a number of scuttling beetles and scorpions, it leaped away in terror and for a long time it showed the greatest fear of a scorpion. After a great deal of coaxing it was at length induced to eat two from which the stings had been removed. It was then shown a third one under a stone and this time it greedily seized the insect and was promptly stung in the palm of the hand. Each kind of wild fruit it handled with the greatest caution, first smelling repeatedly and then nibbling small bits. When it was eventually introduced to the poisonous plants its confidence had grown to such an extent that it plucked and ate a grysappel without hesitation. There was just a little hesitation when it reached the poison plant. It picked a fruit and at once placed the whole of it in its cheek pouch and when it was prevented from picking another, it at once commenced chewing the one it had. It was only then that the sense of taste must have come to the rescue, as the masticated fragments were at once ejected with every sign of distaste and fear, and never after that could our chacma be induced even to handle the leaves or fruit again.

From *The Soul of the Ape*, by Eugene Marais

(a) Why was the otter deliberately kept away from water and prevented from eating fish and crab?

(b) How did it react when it was fully grown and saw water and fish for the first time?

(c) What does this experiment reveal about the instinctive or non-instinctive behaviour of otters?

(d) What is the normal feeding behaviour of South African baboons, displayed even by very small youngsters?

(e) How did the artificially reared baboon react to its natural environment?

(f) What does the experiment reveal about a baboon's instinctive or non-instinctive behaviour?

(g) What other proof is there in this account that a baboon is responsive to learning rather than instinct?

2 *Testing the Close Link between Mother and Offspring*

Much light has been thrown on the nature of this drive by some very interesting experiments recently carried out by Harlow at the University of Wisconsin. He used monkeys for his experiments since these are most closely related to the human species. He was concerned to discover whether the attachment of young monkeys to their mother was the result of her function of supplying an appropriate source of food, whether mother-love was in fact nothing more than cupboard-love.

Harlow prepared two kinds of mother substitutes. The first was constructed of wood, covered with sponge rubber, and sheathed in brown cotton terry cloth. Such a mother was warm and tender, had infinite patience, never scolded and was available twenty-four hours a day.

The second type was constructed of wire and lacked all the soft cuddly properties of the first. Nevertheless, some of the wire mother substitutes were equipped with a very important maternal attribute. They had nipples from which the baby monkeys could be supplied adequately with milk.

He put four baby monkeys in one cage and four in another. In the first cage there was a wire mother with milk and a cloth mother without milk. In the other cage, for comparison, the cloth mother had milk and the wire mother did not.

Harlow and his assistants then watched the behaviour of the baby monkeys in the two cages to see whether they liked the soft cloth mother best or the one with milk.

The results were quite definite. Whether they had milk or not, it was the cloth mothers which were sought by the babies. Apart from the actual feeding time their interest was in being cuddled rather than being near the food supply. They became attached to the cloth mothers and responded to them as to real mothers. When the experimenter brought along a toy bear to frighten them with, eighty per cent of them sought protection from the cloth mother.

Most significant was the behaviour of the baby monkeys when placed in a strange situation, first with the cloth mother, and then without her.

If the cloth mother was there, they would clutch it, rub their bodies against it, and seek the comfort of close contact with it. After a while they would venture away from the cloth mother to explore all the unusual objects in the strange cage, but in between whiles they would go back to the dummy for protection. With it as a base of operations they plucked up sufficient courage to deal with the new and frightening situation and objects around them.

But if the cloth mother was not there with them in the cage, things were quite different. Now there were obvious signs of unhappiness in the baby monkeys. Frequently they would just freeze in a crouched position. Sometimes there was crying, rocking or sucking. Some monkeys would run to the place where the cloth mother had previously been placed and then run from object to object, screaming and crying. The presence of the wire mother did not help and the attitude of the babies to the cloth mother was the same whether or not they were used to getting milk from her . . .

The important point we have to notice about these experiments is that the baby monkeys have a drive which is satisfied only by soft cuddling contact. They instinctively seek for the kind of mothering cuddles and protection which parents instinctively want to give to children. So each encourages the other . . . and children are kept safe until they can look after themselves.

Adapted from *Fundamentals of Psychology*, by Adcock

(a) How did Harlow set up his experiment to test the basis of the attachment of young monkeys to their mothers?

(b) What tests did he carry out?

(c) How did the monkeys respond to these tests?

(d) What did Harlow's findings prove?

(e) Using the evidence of these experiments and assuming that humans respond in much the same way, show what kind of relationship would seem to be the necessary basis for a healthy and happy infancy, as the basis upon which a healthy and happy life can be built.

3 *Anna*

Anna was an illegitimate child whose grandfather strongly disapproved of the mother's indiscretion and who therefore caused the child to be kept in an upstairs room. As a result the infant received only enough care to keep her barely alive. She was seldom moved from one position to another. Her clothing and bedding were filthy. She apparently had no instruction, no friendly attention.

When finally found and removed from the room at the age of nearly six years, Anna could not talk, walk, or do anything that showed intelligence. She was in an extremely emaciated and undernourished condition, with skeleton-like legs and bloated abdomen. She was completely apathetic, lying in a limp supine position and remaining immobile, expressionless, and indifferent to everything. She was believed to be deaf and possibly blind. She of course could not feed herself or make any move on her own behalf. Here, then, was a human organism which had missed nearly six years of socialization. Her condition shows how little her purely biological resources, when acting alone, could contribute to making her a complete person.

By the time Anna died of haemorrhagic jaundice, approximately four and a half years later, she had made considerable progress as compared with her condition when found. She could follow directions, string beads, identify a few colours, build with blocks, and differentiate between attractive and unattractive pictures. She had a good sense of rhythm and loved a doll. She talked mainly in phrases but would repeat words and try to carry on a conversation. She was clean about clothing. She habitually washed her hands and brushed her teeth. She would try to help other children. She walked well and could run fairly well, though clumsily. Although easily excited, she had a pleasant disposition. Her improvement showed that socialization, even when started at the late age of six, could still do a great deal towards making her a person. Even though her development was no more than that of a normal child of two to three years, she had made noteworthy progress.

From *Human Society*, by Kinsley Davis

(a) Anna 'received only enough to keep her barely alive'. Which early learning experiences did she miss?

(b) What effect did this have on Anna by the age of six?

(c) Which particular human characteristics were missing from the child?

(d) Anna was then taken away and given a normal upbringing. What changes did this bring about in the child?

(e) What important conclusions about socialisation can we draw from this case study?

4 *Isabelle*

Isabelle was found at about the same time as Anna under strikingly similar circumstances when approximately six and a half years old. Like Anna, she was illegitimate and had been kept in seclusion for that reason. Her mother was a deaf mute and it appears that she and Isabelle spent most of their time together in a dark room. As a result Isabelle had no chance to develop speech; when she communicated with her mother it was by means of gestures. Lack of sunshine and inadequacy of diet had caused her to become rachitic. Her legs in particular were affected; they were 'so bowed that as she stood erect the soles of her shoes came nearly flat together, and she got about with a skittering gait'. Her behaviour towards strangers, especially men, was almost that of a wild animal, manifesting much fear and hostility. In lieu of speech she made only a strange croaking sound. In many ways she acted like an infant. 'She was apparently utterly unaware of relationships of any kind. When presented with a ball for the first time, she held it in the palm of her hand, then reached out and stroked (the donor's) face with it. Such behaviour is comparable to that of a child of six months.' At first it was even hard to tell whether or not she could hear, so unused were her senses. Many of her actions resembled those of deaf children.

E

Once it was established that she could hear, specialists who worked with her pronounced her feeble-minded. Even on non-verbal tests her performance was so low as to promise little for the future. 'The general impression was that she was wholly uneducable and that any attempt to teach her to speak, after so long a period of silence, would meet with failure.' Yet the individuals in charge of her launched a systematic and skilful programme of training. The task seemed hopeless at first, but gradually she began to respond. After the first few hurdles had at last been overcome, a curious thing happened. She went through the usual stages of learning characteristics of the years from one to six not only in proper succession but far more rapidly than normal. In a little over two months after her first vocalization she was putting sentences together. Nine months after that she could identify words and sentences on the printed page, could write well, could add to ten and could retell a story after hearing it. Seven months beyond this point she had a vocabulary of 1500–2000 words and was asking complicated questions. Starting from an educational level of between one and three years, she had reached a normal level by the time she was eight and a half years old. In short, she covered in two years the stages of learning that ordinarily require six. She eventually entered school where she participated in all school activities as normally as other children.

From Human Society, by Kinsley Davis

(a) Which three human characteristics were particularly undeveloped in the behaviour of Isabelle?

(b) What conclusions did the first experts who contacted Isabelle come to about her behaviour? Why?

(c) What was the real trouble with Isabelle?

(d) Describe *in your own words* the progress she made once a systematic programme of socialisation was begun.

Socialisation and Culture

The kind of learning to be an adult which a child experiences differs, of course, between one culture and another, just as the roles, expectations, and behaviour that goes with adulthood differ in contrasting societies. From the moment a child is born, the sort of contact it has with its immediate environment is a crucial factor in deciding what kind of adult that child will be. As we have already seen among the Tchambuli of New Guinea the sex roles of the society are quite the opposite to our own. The women are the workers, involved in trade and commerce, and are both bossy and aggressive. The men idle around the house, painting, dancing, and flirting, and quite dominated by their wives.

The sorts of characteristics which typify the adults of any society can frequently be traced back to their earliest experiences. Consider, for example, how the first few weeks of life differ considerably in Samoa and among three neighbouring New Guinea tribes:

In Samoa there is no privacy about a birth. Convention dictates that the mother should neither writhe, nor cry out, nor protest at the presence of 20 or 30 people in the house who sit up all night if need be, laughing, joking, and playing games. The midwife cuts the cord with a fresh bamboo knife and then all wait eagerly for the cord to fall off, the signal for a feast. If the baby is a girl, the cord is buried under a paper mulberry tree (the tree from which bark cloth is made) to ensure her growing up to be industrious at household tasks; if a boy it is thrown into the sea so that he may be a skilled fisherman, or planted under a taro plant to make him industrious in farming. Then the visitors go home, the mother rises and goes about her daily tasks, and the new baby ceases to be of much interest to anyone. . . .

Babies are always nursed, and in the few cases where the mother's milk fails her, a wet nurse is sought among the kinsfolk. From the first week they are also given other food – papaya, coconut milk, sugar-cane juice. The food is either chewed by the mother and then put into the baby's mouth on her finger, or if it is liquid a piece of bark cloth is dipped into it and the child allowed to suck it, as shepherds feed orphaned lambs. The babies are nursed whenever they cry and there is no attempt at regularity. Unless a woman expects another child, she will nurse a baby until it is two or three years old, as the simplest device for pacifying its crying. Babies sleep with their mothers as long as they are at the breast; after weaning they are usually handed over to the care of some younger girl in the household. They are bathed frequently with the juice of a wild orange and rubbed with coconut oil until their skins glisten.

From *Coming of Age in Samoa*, by Margaret Mead

The Arapesh treat a baby as a soft, vulnerable, precious little object, to be protected, fed, and cherished. Not only the mother, but the father also, must play this over-all protective role. After birth the father abstains from work and sleeps beside the mother, and he must abstain from intercourse while the child is young, even with his other wife. When the mother walks about, she carries the child slung beneath her breast in a bark-cloth sling, or in a soft net bag in which the child still curls as he curled in the womb. Whenever it is willing to eat even if it does not show any signs of hunger, it is fed, gently and with attention. Through the long, protected infancy during which children are carried slung in bags from their mother's foreheads or high on their father's shoulders up and down the steep mountain trails, they are never asked to perform tasks that are difficult or exacting.

131

The Iatmul believe an unborn child can hurry or delay, as it wishes. 'Why do you rail at me?' said Tchamwole to her husband. 'This baby will be born when it likes. It is a human being, and it chooses its own time of birth. It is not like a pig or a dog to be born when others say it should . . .'

As soon as the Iatmul child is a few weeks old, the mother no longer carries it everywhere with her, or sits with it on her lap, but instead places it at some distance on a high bench, where it must cry lustily before it is fed. Assured that it is hungry, the mother crosses to it and feeds it generously and easily, but a baby that has had to cry hard for its food eats more definitely. Before the baby has any teeth, it is given pieces of hard bird-meat to gnaw on, and when its teeth begin to come in, it cuts them on round shell ornaments that hang around the mother's neck.

The Mundugumor women actively dislike child-bearing, and they dislike children. Children are carried in harsh opaque baskets that scratch their skins, later, high on their mother's shoulders, well away from the breast. Mothers nurse their children standing up, pushing them away as soon as they are the least bit satisfied. Here we find a character developing that stresses angry, eager greed. In later life, love-making is conducted like the first round of a prize-fight, and biting and scratching are important parts of foreplay. When the Mundugumor captured an enemy, they ate him, and laughed as they told of it afterwards. When a Mundugumor became so angry that his anger turned even against himself, he got into a canoe and drifted down the river to be eaten by the next tribe.

From *Male and Female*, by Margaret Mead

Discussion and Written Work

1 (a) What characteristics are highly prized in:
  (i) Samoan girls?
  (ii) Samoan boys?
(b) What is the attitude of Samoan women to feeding and disciplining their babies?
(c) How does the attitude of Arapesh parents differ from that of Samoan parents?
(d) What personality characteristics in later life, do you think, will be developed by the loving relationship with parents of Arapesh children?
(e) What is the Iatmul belief about childbirth?
(f) What is the first lesson learned by Iatmul children?
(g) What effects could this have on the Iatmul child's personality later?
(h) Describe *in your own words* the Mundugumor parent's attitude to children.
(i) In what ways could this affect the child's later relationship:

132

(i) with its parents?

(ii) with other people?

(j) Explain how child-bearing practices in Arapesh and Mundugumor society produce two totally different kinds of adult personalities.

2 From the moment of birth when a little girl is dressed in a pink bonnet, bootees and shawl, and a little boy is dressed in a helmet and romper suit, they begin to learn the different sex roles of our society.

Write an essay to describe how, right from the beginning, we socialise our children to play the accepted male and female roles practised by our society. (You should consider among other things, what sex roles they learn from dress, toys and games, books, songs and rhymes, the mass media, traditional masculine and feminine behaviour and their relationships with their parents.)

3 Discuss together the following passages before attempting the written work:

A. YOUNG GIRLS IN SAMOA

From birth until the age of four or five a child's education is exceedingly simple. They must be house-broken, a matter made more difficult by a habitual indifference to the activities of small children. They must learn to sit or crawl within the house and never to stand upright unless it is absolutely necessary; never to address an adult in a standing position; to stay out of the sun; not to tangle the strands of the weaver; not to scatter the cut-up coconut which is spread out to dry; to keep their scant loin cloths at least nominally fastened to their persons; to treat fire and knives with proper caution; not to touch the kava bowl or the kava cup; and if their father is a chief, not to crawl on his bed place when he is by. These are really simply a series of avoidances, enforced by occasional cuffings and a deal of exasperated shouting and ineffectual conversation.

The weight of the punishment usually falls upon the next oldest child, who learns to shout, 'Come out of the sun', before she has fully appreciated the necessity of doing so herself. By the time Samoan boys and girls have reached 16 or 17 years of age these perpetual warnings to the younger ones have become an inseparable part of their conversation – a monotonous, irritated undercurrent to all their comments. I have known them to interrupt their remarks every two or three minutes with 'Keep still', 'Sit still', 'Keep your mouths shut', 'Stop that noise', uttered quite mechanically although all the little ones present may have been behaving as a row of intimidated mice. On the whole, this last requirement of silence is continually mentioned and never enforced. The little nurses are more interested in peace than in forming the character of their small charges, and

133

when a child begins to howl it is simply dragged out of earshot of its elders. No mother will ever exert herself to discipline a younger child if an older one can be made responsible. Thus each child is being disciplined and socialised through responsibility for a still younger one.

By the time a child is six or seven she has all the essential avoidances well enough by heart to be trusted with the care of a younger child. And she also develops a number of simple techniques. She learns to weave firm square balls from palm leaves, to make pin wheels of palm leaves or frangipangi blossom, to climb a coconut tree by walking up the trunk on flexible little feet, to break open a coconut with one firm well-directed blow of a knife as long as she is tall, to play a number of group games and sing songs which go with them, to tidy the house by picking up the litter on the stony floor, to bring water from the sea, to spread out the copra to dry and to help gather it when rain threatens, to roll the pandanus leaves for weaving, to go to a neighbouring house and bring back a lighted faggot for the chief's pipe or the cookhouse fire, and to exercise tact in begging slight favours from relatives.

But in the case of the little girls all these tasks are secondary to the main business of baby tending. Very small boys also have some care of the younger children, but at eight or nine years of age they are usually relieved of it.

All the irritating routine of housekeeping, which in our civilization is accused of warping the souls and souring the tempers of grown women, is here performed by children under 14 years of age. A fire or a pipe to be kindled, a call for a drink, a lamp to be lit, the baby's cry, any trifling errand of a thoughtless adult – these haunt them from morning until night. With the introduction of several months a year of Government School these children are being taken out of the home for most of the day. This brings about a complete disorganisation of the native households, which have no precedents for a manner of life where mothers have to stay at home and take care of their children and adults have to perform small routine tasks and run errands.

From *Coming of Age in Samoa*, by Margaret Mead

1 Whereabouts is Samoa?
2 What type of society is it?
3 What are the main things a child in Samoa has to learn *not to do* from the time of birth to the age of four or five?
4 Make a list from your own experience of at least six things an English child of the same age must learn not to do.
5 Who is responsible in Samoan society for making sure that the children behave themselves properly?
6 Write a piece to explain how much influence older brothers and sisters have in bringing up children in this country. Are there any differences between middle class and working class homes?

7 What other skills besides baby minding has a Samoan girl learned by the age of six or seven?

8 Why do Samoan girls take on the main responsibility for minding the house, do you think?

9 What effects has 'progress' had on the Samoan girls' responsibilities at home?

10 Write a piece to compare and contrast the life of a Samoan girl of 14 years old with that of a British girl of the same age.

B MANUS CHILDREN

The children are taught neither obedience nor deference to their parents' wishes. A two-year-old child is permitted to flout its mother's humble request that it come home with her. At night the children are supposed to be at home at dark, but this does not mean that they go home when called. Unless hunger drives them there the parents have to go about collecting them, often by force. A prohibition against going to the other end of the village to play lasts just as long as the vigilance of the prohibitor, who has only to turn the back for the child to be off, swimming under water until out of reach.

Manus cooking is arduous and exacting. The sago is cooked dry in a shallow pot stirred over a fire. It requires continuous stirring and is good only for about twenty minutes after being cooked. Yet the children are not expected to come home at meal-time. They run away in the morning before breakfast and come back an hour or so after, clamouring for food. Ten-year-olds will stand in the middle of the house floor and shriek monotonously until someone stops work to cook for them. A woman who has gone to the house of a relative to help with some task or to lay plans for a feast will be assaulted by her six-year-old child, who will scream, pull at her, claw at her arms, kick and scratch, until she goes home to feed him.

The parents who were so firm in teaching the children their first steps have become wax in the young rebels' hands when it comes to any matter of social discipline. They eat when they like, play when they like, sleep when they see fit. They use no respectful language to their parents, and indeed are allowed more licence in the use of obscenity than are their elders. The veriest urchin can shout defiance and contempt at the oldest man in the village. Children are never required to give up anything to parents: the choicest morsels of food are theirs by divine right. They can rally the devoted adults by a cry, bend and twist their parents to their will. They do no work. Girls after they are eleven or twelve, perform some household tasks, boys hardly any until they are married. The community demands nothing from them except respect for property and the avoidance due to shame.

The child in Manus is lord of the universe, undisciplined, unchecked by any reverence or respect for his elders, free except for the narrow thread of shame which runs through his daily life. No other habits of self-control or of self-sacrifice have been laid. It is the typical psychology of the spoiled child. Manus children demand, never give.

From Growing Up in New Guinea, by Margaret Mead

1 Where do the Manus people live?
2 You have already learned something about Manus family life. Explain clearly what is special in Manus society about:
(a) marriage
(b) relationships between husbands and wives
(c) relationships between parents and children
3 Give as many examples from the passage as you can to illustrate how the Manus child displays all the characteristics of a 'spoiled child'.
4 Why do you think the children can be allowed so much freedom to roam around the village as they please without danger?
5 Explain in your own words what are the only two demands the community makes on Manus children.
6 Why do you think the parents are so 'free and easy' with their children?
7 Some children in this country are spoiled and badly behaved, but most parents try to make their children more disciplined than those in the passage. Using the examples in the passage, e.g., running away, demanding food, being rude, etc., show how an English mother would:
(a) expect her child to behave differently
(b) react to this type of behaviour
8 Explain clearly why children who are spoiled or badly behaved in this country behave as they do.

C. WEST INDIANS IN BIRMINGHAM

The typical black child lives with his parents in one or two rooms, usually high up or low down, in a house containing many families, and has little room to play. Because his mother must join the father in earning enough to live the child has to be looked after during the day. He is herded with six to twelve others in a paraffin-heated room and from Monday to Friday knows no mother to love, enjoys no personal attention, never learns from communication and play. At night his mother collects him and puts him to bed early so that she may relax. Her week-ends are spent shopping, cleaning, relaxing. When the ghetto child starts school at five he often seems duller than others: shy, introverted, with a poor vocabulary blurred by dialect and his behavioural pattern confused by the strange life he has led in two homes. He has known two disciplinary codes, and now must adjust to a third at school – that of the white race and middle class. He is prone to be labelled 'problem child', especially by reception teachers unaware of the situations from which children come to them.

From Because They're Black, by Derek Humphry and Gus John

D. BLACK BOY IN HARLEM

This innocent country set you down in a ghetto in which, in fact, it intended that you should perish. Let me spell out precisely what I mean by that, for the heart of the matter is here, and the root of my dispute with my country. You were born where you were born and faced the future that you faced because you were black and *for no other reason*. The limits of your ambition were, thus, expected to be set for ever. You were born into a society which spelled out with brutal clarity, and in as many ways as possible, that you were a worthless human being. You were not expected to aspire to excellence: you were expected to make peace with mediocrity. Wherever you have turned, James, in your short time on this earth, you have been told where you could go and what you could do (and *how* you could do it) and where you could live and whom you could marry. The details and symbols of your life have been deliberately constructed to make you believe what white people say about you. They have had to believe for many years, and for innumerable reasons, that black men are inferior to white men. Many of them, indeed, know better, but, as you will discover, people find it very difficult to act on what they know. To act is to be committed, and to be committed is to be in danger.

From *The Fire Next Time*, by James Baldwin

1 Explain carefully in your own words why the West Indian child in Birmingham is often labelled 'problem child'.
2 What kind of socialisation has white America given to the Negroes of Harlem?
3 Explain with examples the connections between the socialisation experiences of West Indians in Birmingham and Negroes in Harlem.

4 *The Influence of Social Class Sub-Cultures on Socialisation*
Discuss together the evidence in this passage, which was gathered in America, before you do the written work.

Class differences begin in the cradle. Middle-class mothers are likely to make quite a personal drama of being a new mother and lavish their baby with protective love. The working-class mother is likely to have mixed feelings. She'll be matter-of-fact with occasional spontaneous expressions of joyous love.

During the first years of life when personality is largely moulded, youngsters in the lowest class learn to do what comes naturally.

Mothers at the higher level work much harder at training their children to restrain their emotions and to accept responsibilities around the house. Training to 'make good' begins early.

One result of all the training is that at least the middle-class child appears to be more orderly, organized and inhibited than his counterpart in the lower classes. A comparative study of the reactions of four-year-olds of 'middle' and 'lower' classes in the *Boston-Cambridge* area to finger painting is illuminating. The lower-class youngsters dived in, seemed to enjoy messing with the paint. Higher-level youngsters were more inclined to hold back from dabbling in the paint, and when they did they tended to do it daintily.

When toddlers grow into youngsters, the class differences become more clear-cut. Three sociologists focused their scrutiny on a one-half-square-mile area in Chicago that was chosen because it included the whole class gamut of families from real lower to real upper. All the youngsters thus had access to the same community facilities: movies, libraries, playgrounds, Y.M.C.A., Boy Scouts, parks, churches, settlement houses. All children in three year groups of a local school were asked to keep diaries of their daily activities. An analysis of these diaries revealed that, out of school, the youngsters from the lower classes lived in a world largely different from that of the middle classes. After school they went to the clubs and centres specifically designed for the so-called under-privileged. They spent much time at the movies, and they tended to have considerable freedom to roam and to come and go at home.

In contrast, youngsters at the higher level spent much of their time at self-improvement activities such as taking lessons and reading, indicating the future-mindedness of themselves and their parents. And they took part in great numbers in Y.M.C.A. and Boy Scout activities. In *Elmtown*, Hollingshead found the middle classes had ten times as many youngsters in the Boy Scouts as the working class. And in the Girl Guides the proportional representation was about 20 to 1 in favour of the middle classes.

In another investigation, sociologist James West was repeatedly told that 'you don't find any classes here'. Classes were felt to be 'wrong'. And children from better-class homes, he found, were cautioned repeatedly 'never to show' they 'feel any different' from the lower-class youngsters in town. Yet the parents were constantly admonishing the children in ways that showed the differences were very much on their own minds. The parents of the 'better class' warned their children not to play with 'people like that' (lower-class children). For example:

'You don't want to play with Johnny Jones. People like that don't know how to play right. The Jones keep hounds . . . are dirty . . . live back in the timber . . . don't go to church . . . are not *our* kind . . . people would laugh if they saw you at the Jones house.'

The lower-class parents tried their best to prepare their children for the rebuffs they knew would come. They told their youngsters:

'You're just as good as anyone . . . I wouldn't want to go where I wasn't wanted.' Slights received by children are explained with: 'They're stuck up, uppity people . . . cold people . . . they have no manners . . . they're church hypocrites.' And the youngsters are furnished with compensatory thoughts: 'You know how to shoot and trap better than any Smith boy; you could out-fight any Smith boy your size.'

In the disciplining of children, class differences also appear. Among the lower classes, the youngster deemed to be guilty of serious misbehaviour is flogged or deprived of privileges. And the punishment is most likely to be administered by the father. When you get up into the middle classes, the mother is likely to dominate in the disciplining. Father, who typically gets home late from business, is likely to busy himself trying to prove in the few fleeting moments available with children that he is a real pal. At this level, the punishment most commonly inflicted is withdrawal of love.

In cases where the child actually is a bother and a burden to a man and wife because it interferes with their dominant values and compulsions – career, social and economic success, leisure activities – withdrawal of love occurs for prolonged periods, or indefinitely. The child is thrown into a panic and develops guilt feelings. Investigators point out that parents of the middle-classes continually seek to arouse in the child a fear of losing parental love as a technique in training the child and in such a child, a disapproving glance may produce more terror than a twenty-minute lashing.

From *The Status Seekers*, by Vance Packard

(a) (i) What seem to be the basic differences in the behaviour of middle class and working class toddlers?

(ii) Which aspect of their socialisation experience has encouraged this difference?

(b) In what ways do the leisure activities of middle class and working class children differ?

(c) The reasons given by the middle class mother for not playing with Johnny Jones sound typically American. What might a British middle class mother say in the same situation?

(d) The working class parent's rejection of the Smiths is also particularly American. What sort of remarks would a British working class parent make in the same situation?

(e) Explain in your own words the ways in which working class and middle class parents tend to discipline their children.

(f) State with your reasons which points made in the passage could be applied to Britain.

The Mother-Child Relationship

In general, then, the different characteristics of various societies are reinforced by different patterns of child-rearing. If we look at this more

139

closely in our own society, for example, it becomes clear that while all children experience a similar socialisation process to fit them for the cultural demands of being British rather than Chinese or African, Russian or American, there is at the same time a considerable variation in their individual socialisation experiences.

As we have seen, no adult is quite like any other and one principal reason for this is that no person's socialisation experience is quite like anyone else's. Many influences are involved in socialisation, e.g., social class, environment, position in the family, personality of the parents, intelligence and abilities of the child. The first influence which must be taken into account, however, is the nature of the mother-child relationship in the first few years of life when the infant is most dependent, as this extract shows:

From the earliest feeding and handling onwards, a mother has an unremitting influence upon her child's developing personality through the techniques, attitudes and feelings with which she undertakes her maternal role. Over the first few months as he forms his earliest impressions of what the world around him is like, he relates to his mother through sucking, crying, smiling and making sounds and spontaneous movements. If she responds to these warmly and rewardingly he will come to feel that he is loved and acceptable, and his self-expression will expand accordingly. But if her reaction to him is cool, stunted or even resentful and rejecting, then he will come to feel unaccepted, to distrust his own impulses, and the foundations of self-confidence will be missing.

In the months and years that follow, these feelings are reinforced or modified, not only by her, but increasingly by the father and siblings as well. By learning from the ways they respond to him, by identifying with them as models, and by finding ways of coping with the thwartings and conflicts that inevitably confront him, he gradually forms his own particular pattern of adjustment to family life and to himself. Family atmosphere greatly affects this. In general, a warm and permissive one fosters a spontaneous and outgoing child, a cool and impersonal one results in a frustrated, anxious and inhibited child, and an overprotective and possessive one leads to an excessively dependent child.

Right up to the fifth year the mother usually remains the central feature of the child's environment. Her frequent closeness to him is vital, not just for what she can provide for him, but because she comprises a base from which he can explore and adjust to new people and things as they appear on his rapidly widening horizon. How he approaches and responds to them is largely determined by the pattern of his relationship with his mother. If his attachment to her is secure and allows full expression of his developing capacities, he will be positive towards others and eager for new experiences. But if this attachment is full of

140

frustration and anxiety, his relation to others is likely to be characterised by timidity and inhibition, which often conceal pent up aggressive feelings.

From 'The Seven Ages of Man' – Article by Anthony Ambrose

Maternal Deprivation

It is believed to be very necessary for the future well-balanced development of children that they should experience as infants a warm, loving and close relationship with their mother (or if they have no mother, an adult who will act as a mother to them). If the child does not have this relationship, this is called maternal deprivation. Often children who are delinquent, or who seem to have no feelings for anyone, or whose behaviour is difficult, have experienced maternal deprivation in their early years.

Here in brief are the typical characteristics of children who have experienced maternal deprivation:

1 inability to make deeper emotional relationships
2 no real feeling – no capacity to care for people or to make true friends
3 unable to be reached – annoying and frustrating for those trying to help
4 no emotional response to situations where such a response would be normal – a curious lack of concern
5 deceit and evasion – often pointless
6 stealing
7 lack of concentration in school

Leaving Mother

The process of socialisation does not stop after the first vital years of learning, but continues throughout the child's life. The first agent of socialisation, as we have seen, is the mother, and then gradually the rest of the child's immediate family. But as the size and experiences of the child's world increase, so do the influences upon him.

In a pre-industrial society, socialisation is carried on by the wider kinship group who by word, deed, and attitude teach the child the norms of his community.

In a society like ours, the agencies of socialisation are more numerous. As soon as the child begins to play out in the street and form friendships with other children, he is exposed to a different type of relationship from that in the family and a different social role has to be learned. When he goes to school, he will again come into contact with a different social atmosphere in which certain expectations are held about him and in which he will have to learn to perform appropriately. From this time on, as he moves in and out of differing social groups and situations, he will be constantly socialised into the behaviour of these groups and situations and constantly adapting himself to cope with new social roles. From schoolboy to husband, from

141

apprentice to foreman, from father to grandfather, and in all his other roles, the behaviour demanded has already been decided by society: he has merely to learn it.

As a backcloth to all of this, there exists the legal framework of society, with laws and regulations to be learned; there is the established moral code of society, which provides the structure of beliefs, attitudes, and socially acceptable behaviour to be followed; and there are the mass media to hand out information, influence and opinion, to affect, as never before, the individuals social development.

The Peer Group

The peer group is the name given by sociologists to the group of friends of a similar age with whom children spend a lot of their time. There is often conflict between the standards of family and those of peers. For example, a fourteen-year-old wrote in his diary:

I came home from school and had my tea. My mum knocked a flowerpot off the window ledge and asked me to sweep it up for her. I took out the dust-pan and brush and started to clear up, but then my mate Arthur came along and he said I was cissy to help my mum, so I stopped. I went with Arthur over to the flats where he lives and we met our other mates.

The boys often share with each other attitudes to stealing and other forms of delinquency that their parents do not hold. They also follow each other, and adolescent fashions generally, in things like dress, hairstyles and tastes in music.

There is another way in which the peer group exerts an important influence. Within it the adolescent boy can enjoy a freedom and equality he cannot find at school, at work, or inside his family. This sense of fraternity is often mentioned:

'You can be yourself with your mates,' boys say. They stress the sense of liberation: 'I like going out with the boys. You can have a laugh.' 'We always have a giggle when we're together.'

They sometimes recognise also how this mood could lead to wildness and 'hooliganism':

(a) 'When you're by yourself you're quite tame,' a 16-year-old commented. 'When you're with a mob, it's quite different.'

142

(b) 'When you're in a group, you get kind of excited,' said a 17-year-old. 'You get carried away. You do things you wouldn't do on your own – smash things up, just for a laugh, or cheek some old man, or fight some other kids.'

(c) A 15-year-old thought that the habit of destructiveness started at an early age. 'When you're a little kid, you smash up the things people chuck on the bomb sites, like old baths, old prams, old boxes and that. And motor-cars – there's always old motor vans on the bomb sites that the kids smash up. At first they think the bits they pull off are going to be useful for something, but when they get them off there's always something wrong with them, say some bracket won't come off, so then they do some more smashing up. It goes in crazes. After that we used to smash up builders' boards and "House to Let" notices. We didn't do it very much, but I know for a time we was pulling up those "House to Let" boards, and we used to dump them in the canal or in the Victoria Park Lake. I don't know why we did it; it was for a giggle.'

From *Adolescent Boys of East London*, by Peter Willmott

Peer groups do not always exert a bad influence on young people, however, since high spirits do not always end in hooliganism or destructiveness.

Discussion and Written Work

1 PROJECT: CHILD STUDIES

Make a careful study of a child in an environment where you can observe him/her closely over a period of time. When you compare these studies in class, it will be possible to discuss the types of behaviour that are fairly typical of children of a certain age group and also the ways in which some children differ. Perhaps you will be able to suggest reasons why individual children behave as they do.

Before you begin your child study, find out which age group the child is in and follow the appropriate guide (given below). Also, be sure to note down some details about the child's background. When the study is complete, write a clear and logical account of your findings. Be sure to cover in detail all the points in the guide.

A. AGE-GROUP: 0 TO 18 MONTHS

Preliminary Notes

1 Name

2 Age

3 Number in family

4 Child's position in the family

5 Description of where the family lives

143

1 How many inches does the child measure? How much does it weigh?
2 Does the child cry very much? At what particular times does it cry?
Can you give any reasons for its crying?
3 How does the child's mother behave when it cries? Does she:
(a) pick it up immediately?
(b) leave it to cry?
(c) sometimes pick it up, sometimes leave it?
4 How does the child respond when its parents pick it up? What happens
when a stranger picks it up?
5 Is the child timid and frightened, or friendly and unconcerned, in the
presence of strange adults?
6 How does the child respond when you touch its hand or put a small
object (say a clothes peg) into his hand? Try this test with other objects
and see if the child's behaviour is the same.
7 What happens when the child hears a sudden noise?
8 Does the child play with toys very much? What sort of toys does it seem
to prefer? What happens if you take its toys away?
9 Can the child talk? If not, what sort of sounds does it make? If so, what
words does it say? Can it say whole sentences?
10 Is the child toilet-trained yet?
11 Can the child feed itself or does it need help from its mother?
12 Describe the sort of movements made by the child when it is on the
floor. Can it walk yet?

B. AGE GROUP: 18 MONTHS TO 3 YEARS
Preliminary Notes
1 Name
2 Age
3 Number in family
4 Position in family
5 Description of where the family lives

1 How many inches does the child measure? How much does the child
weigh?
2 Does the child cry very much? What are its main reasons for crying – is
it angry, hurt, afraid, uncomfortable, or annoyed because it cannot do
something?
3 How does the child's mother react when it cries? Does she get angry,
worried, try to bribe it to be good with offers of sweets, etc., or does she
try to soothe it by talking to it for a while?
4 How does the child respond to strangers? Is it timid and shy, or friendly
and unafraid?

5 Can the child tell the difference between different colours? Try some experiments to test the child's knowledge of colour.

6 (a) Is the child an only child? If so, see how it behaves with other children. Is it selfish with its toys? Is it frightened by other children?

(b) Is the child one of a small family? If so, does it play with its brothers and sisters very much? How do they behave together?

(c) Is the child one of a large family? If so, does it play with its brothers and sisters very much? How do they behave together? Do any of them share the responsibility with mother for looking after the child?

7 What sorts of toys and games does the child prefer? Does it have a favourite toy?

8 Can the child talk? What words does it say? Can it speak in sentences? Give examples of the sorts of phrases and sentences it uses.

9 Can the child feed itself? If so, describe the way in which it does this.

10 Is the child toilet-trained yet?

11 Can the child walk yet? Describe the sorts of movements it makes on the floor.

12 Do the child's parents spend much time reading or telling stories to the child?

13 Is the child well behaved and obedient to its parents' wishes, or does it often refuse to behave as it is told?

C. AGE GROUP: 3 YEARS TO 5 YEARS

Preliminary Notes

1 Name

2 Age

3 Number in family

4 Position in family

5 Description of where the family lives

1 How tall is the child? How much does the child weigh?

2 Does the child cry very much? What are the main reasons for its crying – is it hurt, angry, afraid, or annoyed because it cannot do something?

3 How does the child's mother react when it cries? Does she get angry, worried, try to bribe it to be good with offers of sweets, etc., or does she try to sooth it by talking to it for a while?

4 How does the child respond to strangers? Is it timid and shy, or friendly and unafraid?

5 Does the child like to play with other children, or does it play happily on its own?

6 Does the child get angry easily? If so, what sorts of things make it angry?

7 Does the child talk very much? Does it ask a lot of questions?

8 How do the child's parents react to its questions – do they get impatient or do they try to answer all the questions fully? How does the child behave if the questions aren't answered?

9 Is the child well behaved and obedient to its parents' wishes, or does it often refuse to behave as it is told?

10 What kinds of toys and games does the child prefer? Does it have a favourite toy?

11 Does the child like to choose which clothes it will wear, or doesn't it mind?

12 How does the child behave in the presence of strangers? Does it like to show off and seek attention?

13 Do the child's parents spend much time reading to the child or telling it stories? What kinds of books, if any, does the child like?

14 Is the child able to read or write at all yet?

2 The following is an account of an eight-year-old girl who had been adopted a year and a half before this extract was written:

After an illegitimate birth, the child was shifted about from one relative to another, finally brought to a child-placing agency, and then placed in a foster-home for two months before she came to the adoptive parents. The complaints were lying and stealing. The parents described the child's reaction to the adoption as very casual. When they took her home and showed her the room she was to have all for herself, and took her on a tour of the house and grounds, she showed apparently no emotional response. Yet she appeared very lively and 'affectionate on the surface'. After a few weeks of experience with her, the adoptive mother complained to her husband that the child did not seem able to show any affection. The child, to use the mother's words, 'would kiss you but it would mean nothing'. The husband told his wife that she was expecting too much, that she should give the child a chance to get adapted to the situation. The mother was somewhat comforted by these remarks, but still insisted that something was wrong. The father said he saw nothing wrong with the child. In a few months, however, he made the same complaint. By this time, also, it was noted that the child was deceitful and evasive. All methods of correction were of no avail. . . . The school-teacher complained of her general inattention and her lack of pride in the way her things looked. However, she did well in her school subjects, in keeping with her good intelligence. She also made friends with children though none of these were close friendships. After a contact of a year and a half with the patient the adoptive father said, 'You just can't get to her', and the mother remarked, 'I have no more idea to-day what's going on in that child's mind than I knew the day she came. You can't get under her skin. She never tells what she's thinking or what she feels. She chatters but it's all surface.'

From *Child Care and the Growth of Love*, by John Bowlby

(a) Give examples from the passage to show how far the girl displays the typical characteristics of maternally deprived children.

(b) Which types of children are likely to suffer from maternal deprivation, do you think?

(c) Write a piece to say why you think that children deprived of love and affection and a motherly relationship when they are young should behave like the girl in the passage as they grow older.

(d) When the girl grows up and gets married herself, how do you think her childhood experiences will affect:

(i) her relationship with her husband?

(ii) her relationship with her children?

3 Write an essay to explain the ways in which a child's relationship with its mother affects its future relationships with other people.

4 *Shirley*

This is taken from the diary of a student teacher – she has paid a visit to the home of one of her pupils:

Shirley invited Una and me to tea at her home in answer to my suggestion that she should decide what we were going to do this week. I arrived at about twenty to three and was met off the bus by Shirley and Una. We trotted round to their house – Shirley dragging along a rather reluctant dog and talking excitedly all the way. Inside, the house was rather dilapidated and tatty and filled with junk – though it was obvious that some rapid clearing up had been done in my honour, as piles of magazines and various bits and pieces had been stuffed under and behind armchairs. Although the place was tatty there obviously wasn't any shortage of money. There was a huge gramophone and television (twenty-three inch screen, as I was told), with a large electric fire belting out heat at a phenomenal rate.

Shirley's mother was very pleasant, though she was obviously a little ill at ease at first. She was quite interested in what I was doing but was far more concerned to tell me what a gay life she led! This involved looking at hundreds of photographs showing 'me marrying our dad' to 'me getting drunk at Brighton'.

She was obviously very fond of her two little sons who were very quiet and shy at first – but she was unable to cover up the friction that exists between her and Shirley. For example, Shirley spilt some of her tea in her saucer and got a

147

very sharp telling-off for her lack of manners! But when one of the boys tipped a whole cupful all over the carpet his mother found it highly amusing. Shirley was quick to point out the difference in her attitude toward her.

Both Shirley and her mother are very quick-tempered, over-critical and rather petulant. Obviously they are too much alike to get on well together. They were constantly correcting each other and getting impatient with each other. My presence acted as a restraint and Shirley's mother was obviously trying not to lose her temper with her or to give me a bad impression of their relationship. However Shirley was aware of this also and refused to play the game!

At about 3.30 Mrs Jenkins left to go to work. She kissed the two boys before going and then on sudden inspiration decided to kiss Shirley also! Shirley's reaction was ' 'ere, what you doing – you've never done that before – go away'. Obviously she felt her mother was being rather a fraud and did her best to thwart her attempts.

After her mother had gone Shirley came into her own right! She became rather excited and boastful and started to boss the two boys around. When the little one wet his pants both Una and I were rather surprised at the vehemence of her reaction. She shoved him out of the room very harshly, complaining bitterly and hitting him hard. She obviously resents very much having to look after the two boys so much and also her mother's preferential treatment of them. Accordingly she feels very little affection for them and treats them much as her mother treats her. It's a bit of a vicious circle as apparently Shirley's eldest brother is always hitting her, and she dislikes all her brothers to quite an extent.

From *Young Teachers and Reluctant Learners*, by Hannam,
Stephenson and Smyth

(a) Describe Shirley's house in your own words.

(b) Suggest a street near to the area of the school where such a house might be found.

(c) Use four examples from the passage to describe Shirley's relationship with her mother.

(d) (i) Give three examples of the ways in which Mrs Jenkins tried to impress the student teacher.

(ii) Why do you think she did this?

(e) (i) Why might Shirley feel annoyed by the way she is treated at home?

(ii) How does she react to this?

(f) Say with your reasons which of the following statements most accurately applies to Shirley's family:

(i) the children are strictly brought up.

(ii) there is little evidence of love in the house.

(iii) the parents are separated.

(iv) the family is reasonably happy – it's just that as a unit they don't work very well.

5 *Charlie Smith*

(There are many men like Charlie Smith – repeatedly in trouble, repeatedly in court, repeatedly in and out of prison. Their crimes and their lives are equally hopeless and unsuccessful. Many of their childhood experiences are strikingly similar too. Here is Charlie Smith's own account.)

In my life, do you mean, what's the first thing I ever remember? Well I should say it's being in the house, like, with the family, and getting thrown through the air onto me cot, and crying me head off. Me dad and me uncles were celebrating I should think, you know, drinking and that, and I remember going through the air, being thrown, and frightened, and landing like that on me face in the cot. I don't know how old I was, can't have been very old, perhaps two or something like that, I should think, if I was being thrown into a cot . . .

From what I've heard, my mother was an old-fashioned, timid sort of woman, very – you know, as a mother should be to her children, homely and lovable and things like that. I think she must have went through a hard time with me father, you know, because he used to drink such a lot, him and me uncles were always celebrating, drinking and singing in the house. She had to do all the work, all the heavy work like getting the coal and the washing, feeding them, clearing up, and putting up with a lot of swearing and rudeness from them too. People who've spoke of her, it was always like they were sorry for her because of what she had to go through, and they said me father always kept her short of money because he spent such a lot himself on the drink.

He was in the mines, I think, and in them days his wages can't have been all that much. I think he was a bit of a gambler too, liked to bet on the horses now and again. I've got no kind of feeling about him at all and yet sometimes I think in a way I must be like him, specially where the drinking's concerned, anyway.

The first time I ever knew I was an orphan was not till I was about six or seven. Up till then I'd lived in the Cottage Homes of the County Council. I remember them as being a bit rough, I was always hungry and getting smacked. We lived in a kind of group, all together under one woman that we all called 'Mother', about twenty children altogether, I should think. There were several houses with the same number of kids in each, all grouped together, you know, like a sort of colony on its own.

Well, when I was nearly seven I went on from the Cottage Homes and into the orphanage, and, like I say, it was there I first got to know how I was fixed.

149

It was a Roman Catholic orphanage, of course, and we were looked after by the Sisters. One day in the playground we were sitting on the ground in a corner listening to one of them telling us a story about a boy who hadn't got any mother or father. When she'd finished I hung around near her for a bit and then I went up to her and said: 'Sister, where's my mother and father?' And she said: 'Your mother and father's both dead, son. That's why you're here, because you're an orphan, like all the others.' . . .

The Sisters looked after us and clothed and fed us, but they were strict. Every morning one of them used to come round the dormitory pulling back the bedclothes to wake us up, and also look for anyone who'd wet his bed in the night. We nearly all of us did at one time or another, not through laziness but because we just didn't know we'd done it, the first thing you knew was off would come the bedclothes, and then you'd get a terrific clout on the head. You had to go straight to the bathroom and have a cold bath, whether it was summer or winter. One of the big boys was in charge of the bath, and he'd have it full right up with cold water. In you'd get, shivering and crying, and he'd push you right down into it, pushing you under as many times as he liked and thought you deserved. Then you had to run stark naked back to the dormitory to dry yourself and get dressed, and on the way the Sister would be waiting for you and she gave you a stinging slap on the behind and told you what a dirty boy you were.

I stayed at the orphanage until I was about nine, and then I was taken by a lady called Mrs Waters to live with her in a village near where I'd lived after I was born.

This Mrs Waters had quite a few children of her own, about five or six, I think it was, with a boy of my own age called Terry who became my particular pal. All the others were older than him, so I should think Mrs Waters thought I'd be company for Terry. Him and me used to get up to all sorts of pranks like boys do, scrumping apples from the orchards round about, and all things like that. We played football together, and we went to the same school, and we both played in the football team, me at inside-left and Terry on the wing.

Then the next thing that happened – a good bit after, this was – I was just getting ready for school one morning at Mrs Waters' when a man came to the front door and said he'd come to take me away to live somewhere else. And she says: 'Yes that's right, Charlie,' she says, and then she bursts into tears and I started crying too. 'What have I done?' I says. 'Why are you sending me away?' But she didn't explain or tell me anything, just went on crying and told me I'd better hurry up, and get me things together. He took me on a bus somewhere, quite a long journey it was, and took me to another house, where the woman says: 'Oh you've brought him, have you?' and she took me in, and I never saw Mrs Waters or Terry again.

This other woman, she was called Mrs Thorley, I don't know how long I stayed with her, but after a time she said she was going to ask for more money for me from the Ministry or whoever it was, and they can't have paid it because I was taken away from her and put with someone else, another woman in another town altogether. Her, I can't even remember her name, so I can't have been there very long, but I remember one day a man came to the house and said he was from the people who paid the money for me to be looked after. He asked me had I ever thought what I wanted to be, and I said yes, I'd like to be a farmer. He said well it was about time I was thinking about what I was going to be as I was getting to be a big lad, and I ought to think about it. Then he said: 'Well come on now, sonny, now's your big chance, I'm taking you to Liverpool, so pack your things up and let's get off.'

I kept asking him questions about what sort of a place we were going to in Liverpool, was it a farm and all things like that, and he said it was a sort of school where they taught you to be something for when you grew up, and I was going to like it and it was a big chance for me.

When I got there it was only a few days before I found out it had got nowt to do with me being a farmer, it was just another orphanage, where lads went to when they were about the age I was, eleven or twelve, and while they were there they were taught a trade, and farming didn't come into it at all.

From *The Unknown Citizen*, by Tony Parker

(a) What are Charlie's earliest impressions of family life?

(b) From what you have learned about the significance of those early years of infancy, what effects would you expect this experience to have on his later development?

(c) Do you think Charlie's drinking was a characteristic inherited from his father or the result of something else? What *sociological* reasons can you give for your answer?

(d) Although Charlie had a woman who acted as 'mother' to him at the Cottage Homes, show how, in fact, he was suffering from maternal deprivation.

(e) Do you think the orphanage provided a good atmosphere for a child to grow up in? Give full reasons for your answer.

(f) What is one of the main clues in Charlie's behaviour as a child that he was severely disturbed?

(g) Although Mrs Waters seems to have been quite kind, Charlie's experiences of foster parents are not very satisfactory. Give three illustrations from the passage to show the inadequacies of his foster-upbringing.

(h) How was Charlie 'tricked' into going into the second orphanage? What effect would yet another disappointment like this have on him in the future do you think?

6 (a) What is meant by the term 'peer group'?

(b) Suggest some examples from your own knowledge or experience in which the influence of peer groups has had a good effect on young people.

(c) In what ways does the peer group affect a youngster's dress, taste in music, hobbies, and interests?

Chapter 9

Housing

Unit 1: Slum Housing

Slums

There are decaying areas in every large city. These contain considerable numbers of people living in sub-standard conditions which are grossly inadequate. Often the houses are in closely packed cheek-by-jowl terraces, built quickly and cheaply in the mid and late nineteenth century to cater for the workers in industry. A hundred years later, eaten away by decay, they are still being inhabited by working class, low-income tenants, waiting for redevelopment. One such community lives in the St Ann's area of Nottingham:

St Ann's is a slum. It is a slum which crawls on, wearily, over more than three hundred of Nottingham's dirtiest acres and more than eighty of its greediest years. The money which has been sucked out of the people of St Ann's has accomplished remarkable improvements in the suburbs of Nottingham and even further afield. At least one of the landlords of the first sector scheduled for clearance had an address in Cannes. But St Ann's itself has just gone on and on, and down and down.

The living conditions in St Ann's, as we shall see, are very poor. The rents are low, but they provide a steady 'unearned' income for the absentee landlords living in middle class suburbia or even abroad.

In London, accommodation is often in the rented rooms of large, crumbling, once magnificent Victorian houses. As many as three or four families, often more, live in these houses, sharing the facilities of bathroom and toilet with all the other tenants. These are also slums.

In Glasgow, one third of the houses are unfit for human habitation. Many of them are tenements or large blocks of flats, again built as long as a hundred years ago.

The slums exist because no government has yet been able to conquer the housing shortage in this country. Not only do we need new houses to keep pace with the growing population, we also need vast redevelopment schemes to rehouse the people at present living in old and delapidated slum remnants of the last century. These people, because of poverty, lack of job

153

security, and the high cost of private housing, cannot afford to buy their own homes. Some experts have argued that in 1971 the cost of 80% of new houses was beyond the reach of 90% of the population, and while some can afford to buy older and cheaper houses, the majority have to wait for local and central government action.

Amenities

The three basic amenities to make a house pleasant to live in are: an inside lavatory; a bathroom; and a hot-water system. In St Ann's the figures are these:

	%		%
Lavatory	Inside 9.0	Outside	91.0
Bathroom	Yes 15.0	No	85.0
Hot-water system	Yes 45.5	No	54.5

The lavatories are most frequently found at the end of the yard. Apart from their inconvenience and discomfort during the wintry weather, they present very real difficulties. People who are old and frail find the journey down the yard and back both time-consuming and physically exhausting, and, in icy conditions, actually dangerous.

When the only source of water is the kitchen tap, the kitchen sink has to be used not only for washing up kitchen utensils, but also for preparing food, washing and shaving, and laundry. This is an insanitary and awkward arrangement, made even more difficult for those who do not have a hot-water supply. They have to boil a kettle every time they need warm water, and that is an expensive business as well as an inconvenient one. At bathtime out comes the tin tub in front of the fire. The effort required to fill this, working from saucepans on a gas stove, can only be assessed by those who have done it, as this account shows:

There was always a palaver in our kitchen on a Friday night. At exactly eight o'clock the curtains were drawn and every possible container – kettles, bowls, pans – was filled to the brim with cold water. I had to watch they didn't boil over on the cooker while Mum went downstairs and out into the back-yard to struggle all the way up with the big tin bath.

I always felt sorry for that tin bath. All the week it hung outside on the shed door, neglected in all weathers. On a rainy night we were kept awake with the monotonous tune of drops tap-dancing and drumming on it, but still it hung there, rain-rusted and speckled white with bird droppings. However, once a week it was brought into the warm kitchen and there, for a few hours, it was fussed over like a new-born babe. It was welcomed upstairs only, though, for downstairs I heard the sound of bass booming as it banged against furniture and corners.

'Christ Almighty, Vi, mind the Old Man's head.'

And all the way up the stairs Grandad swore and Mum apologised.

'It gets bigger and noisier every week,' Mum panted as the bath entered the door and filled our steaming kitchen. Look out, that water's boiling over. Now you get ready. I'm all behind tonight, you'll have to be quick.'

I stood on a chair and undressed while Mum cleaned out the bath, but it was so big and took such a long time that it was never done properly. I got used to sitting on the gritty bottom and always expected to see a couple of drowned spiders floating on the surface.

By this time there was so much steam in the kitchen I could hardly see Mum lift off the containers to pour them in the bath.

'Mind out or you'll get splashed!' she screamed, her voice almost drowned by the great gushing hot waterfall.

When the bath was filled enough so that the water would at least cover my legs, Ibcol and soda were thrown in, and then it was ready to receive me.

On toe in: 'OUCH! Ooh, it's too hot, Mum. Put in some cold.' Only a basinful was thrown in because Mum had to come in after me while it was still hot. The worst part about having a bath was sitting down.

'Will you stop messing about? We haven't got all night and you're making that water cold.'

When I wasn't looking Mum pushed my bottom down and before I could scream, I found I was in. There was no time to enjoy the luxury of warm water, for to Mum bathing was a business, not a pleasure. She washed my back while I was supposed to wash my front, but I liked to blow bubbles.

'You can stop that lark, Valerie. I've told you to hurry up. As if we haven't got enough soap and water over the floor already. Be all right if it's dripping onto the Old Man's head downstairs, wouldn't it? Now have you washed yourself properly?'

No sooner was I up than Mum started rubbing me down red. While I put on my clean pyjamas that had been cooked hot on the oven door, more hot water was added, then it was Mum's turn to bath.

Then we used the same containers to empty the water into the slop bucket. Bucket after bucket was taken downstairs until the bath was empty. This usually ended up with me getting soaked and having to put on another pair of pyjamas. It was fatal to leave an important letter lying on the table. Mum did once and found all the words had run into one another, making gorgeous blue tributaries; she hadn't read it, so she pretended the letter had got lost in the post.

Mum put on her coat and pushed the clean bath out of the door and I felt sad as I heard it booming downstairs as if singing down the musical scale because

I thought it would be ages till the next week when I would hear it singing up the scale.

While Mum took it downstairs I mopped up the pools of water and talcum powder; the steam had now dissipated. Tears trickled down the mirror and the walls perspired. When Mum came back I went downstairs to say good night before going to bed.

From London Morning, by Valerie Avery

Examples of Slum Housing Conditions

A. ST ANN'S, NOTTINGHAM

In St Ann's there are 10,000 houses crushed into an area of about 340 acres at a rate of something like 40 houses per acre compared with 12 houses per acre on more recently built council-housing estates. They are small, two-up and two-down with an attic, and housing a population of 62.6 people per acre compared with 17 people per acre in Nottingham as a whole.

The attic rooms are usually the first to go: they are normally exceptionally difficult to heat, and are often, therefore, extremely damp, even when the roof is sound. In some cases, rain pours in, to be trapped in a whole battery of pails and cans; in others, the ceilings have fallen, the plaster is leaving the walls, the woodwork is powdered away. In one house you could see daylight in the attic, not through the roof (where it is a fairly common sight) but through the wall itself: the plaster had fallen away, leaving a chink between the bricks through which a very healthy sunbeam frisked. Closer examination showed that this attic's outer wall was only one brick thick. Exactly a quarter of the houses had one or more rooms which were considered by their inhabitants to be unusable.

In one case, for example, the floorboards in an upstairs bedroom were so rotten that on two occasions a leg of the bed had broken through the floor, and burst through the plaster of the ceiling below. One lady said that when she was making the bed upstairs her foot went right through the floor, and there she sat, hollering for help, with her leg waving about through the living-room ceiling.

Another house had, in its main living-room, a wooden window-frame which had so deteriorated that it was in constant danger of falling away from the masonry; it was tenuously held in place with string. The window itself could not be opened with any confidence; but fortunately, the cracks between the frame and wall ensured a constant supply of fresh air. In all these cases, the rooms concerned had to be used because of the acute shortage of space their abandonment would have produced.

The major cause of such poor conditions is natural decay through age: the houses were none too carefully finished when they were built and they have long reached the end of their useful life. In many cases the very brickwork is powdered with age; it crumbles beneath the fingers when touched. The pointing between the bricks has often flaked away, leaving a delicate tracery of corrosion through which the wind and rain find ways to continue their work of destruction. The slates on the roof-tops are frequently cracked or broken, and many of them are missing. Rusted guttering and fractured drainpipes sag and lean around some houses, pitching water down the sides of their outer walls, to mark out its own mouldy patterns in the reeking patches which appear indoors. Rot, in any of its forms, and sometimes in several together, visits the woodwork. Often, neither doors nor windows will open properly, or shut again once opened.

Cockroaches, mice and rats all find comfortable resting grounds. The rats come up from the sewers, which are in no better condition than the houses. Some of the feeder sewers were built of bricks and the same decline of solidity which has set in among the houses has also, apparently, been under way beneath the ground. As the old bricks rot away, the sewers collapse, not only frightening the rats, but blocking the pipes and, in wet seasons, causing floods. Some people complained not only that their cellars had been filled with evil-smelling effluent, but that on especially bad days their backyards had been overrun by sewage.

From *Poverty – The Forgotten Englishmen*, by Coates and Silburn

B. NOTTING HILL, LONDON

There are 200,000 more families than there are houses in Greater London which means overcrowding and slum dwelling. About the worst housing conditions are to be found in Notting Hill, Kensington. The Medical Officer of Health of Kensington and Chelsea described a typical house like this:

A typical example of an individual house in bad multiple occupation is a large five-storey and basement dwelling in this area. In three storeys there were 11 lettings with a weekly income of £27 from the 24 occupants. For their use only two water closets and two sinks were provided. No piped hot water supply existed and the communal bathroom and one of the two common sinks were quite unusable. In the former the wash basin had been removed and the remains of a broken geyser, a large tin bath full of stagnant and offensive dirty water, together with other rubbish, filled the bath. The floor was littered with liquor bottles, paper cartons and sundry rubbish. 'The kitchen contained two filthy unusable cookers and an enormous collection of foul and dirty milk bottles filling a large packing case. The entrance hall and staircase were in a particularly dirty condition. Clearly no cleansing of floors, walls or ceilings had been carried out for a very long time. Two external balconies at the front of the house were filled to parapet level with long-standing accumulation of offensive refuse, discarded cans and bottles. All the electric switches or ceiling fittings in the common parts were unusable – either wrenched out, damaged or dangling. In many of the flats trailing flexes inexpertly fixed to the heating, lighting or cooking appliances constituted a serious hazard. Incidentally two rooms were in part-time occupation as a day nursery, apparently in conjunction with the brothel which operated on the premises.'

At all ages from the unborn infant to the old-age pensioner these bad aspects of multi-occupation obviously have a bad influence. As always, it is difficult to give a statistical proof, but one only has to think of an infant, a toddler, a school child or a teenager, compelled to live in such an environment, to realise how adverse the influence must be, particularly on mental and moral health.

The herding of people, often incompatible, the inadequate and inconvenient washing, sanitary and food handling facilities, stairs, noise, fetching and carrying distances, and the dirt, dilapidation and depressing appearance resulting from the neglect of parts used in common, all have their effects.

To those must be added the increased liability to home accidents, infections, contagion, risk of fire and mental stress.

C. GLASGOW

80,000 families in Glasgow are on the council waiting list. 100,000 (one third) of its houses are unfit for human habitation, and 72,510 (23.8%) of its households have no hot water tap. 187,890 people (19.8%) are overcrowded.

In Glasgow, not long ago, a house in the Gorbals was condemned. 58 people were discovered to be living in three flats comprising four rooms each. In the first were a family of ten, a family of seven, and an old man. In the second were a family of six, of three, of six, of four, and an elderly couple. In the third were families of six, eight and five. All cooked on their coal fires.

There was one cold tap in each flat. None of the toilets was working and buckets of water had to be taken on each visit. There were bugs and rats and the house was in a state of unspeakable squalor. Four of the girls and three of the boys ran away from the nightmare of overcrowding and decay.

Discussion and Written Work

1 Look at the census information for your area:
(a) What percentage of the households in your area lack the basic household amenities?
(b) Are there any particular parts in which household amenities are poorer than average? What type of areas are these?
(c) On an outline map of your area mark in the parts:
    (i) which have the most households lacking two or more basic amenities.
    (ii) which have the least households lacking two or more basic amenities.
(d) What conclusions can you draw about household amenities from your completed map?

158

2 Describe as fully and as realistically as you can the living conditions typical of slum houses. (Use examples from your reading and your own knowledge.)

3 Do you think that owners are concerned about slum premises? Give your reasons fully, with examples from the passages to illustrate your answer.

4 Suggest reasons to explain why slum tenants allow their houses to become so filthy.

5 Why do you think that living conditions like these are bad for:
(a) young children?
(b) teenagers?
(c) elderly people?

6 Are there any areas in your city which compare with St Ann's? Try to arrange to visit such an area, make notes, then answer these questions:
(a) When were the houses built?
(b) What sort of people were they built for and who lives there now?
(c) Are the houses privately owned or do the tenants pay rent to a private landlord?
(d) Is there any evidence of rats and mice?
(e) Is there any evidence of decay? Go on to describe in detail the condition of the houses.
(f) Is the landlord willing to do repairs?
(g) Is the area scheduled for redevelopment?

Unit 2: The Neighbourhood

Twilight Zones

The deprived and delapidated areas of industrial towns where slum conditions persist are called twilight zones. Areas like these produce their own social problems. The following passage shows the harmful effects to young children of living in a twilight zone.

For millions of children growing up in Britain life is still a matter of relative poverty. Professor Peter Townsend has reported that between seven and eight million people, or about 4 per cent of the total population live below a specifically defined 'national assistance' standard. As these lower-income groups often have the largest families, it could be that something like one-fifth of the child population of Britain grows up in an environment that in certain fundamental respects can be classed as 'deprived'.

Some of these neighbourhoods have for generations been starved of new schools, new houses and new investment of every kind. Everyone knows this; but for year after year priority has been given to the new towns and new suburbs, because if new schools do not keep pace with the new houses some children will be unable to go to school at all.

A primary school head teacher, talking about children in such areas said this:

'Do you know, we even have to teach some of these children how to play. When they first come here they sit around with vacant expressions. Communication by them and with them is non-existent. In the Infants, we get some children that aren't even toilet-trained – at five! In twilight areas, nursery schools are almost essential. Contact between the children and people other than their parents cannot start young enough.'

The head teacher went on to explain some of the problems of running a school in such an area.

'The kind of teaching we need is different with these children, too, as their mothers have never told them bedtime stories. They need to be told stories very frequently. In this way they become more interested in books and ask to see the pictures. Then they want to talk about the pictures and plenty of time should be allowed for this. Many, coming from homes where parents have no time to talk to them or take any interest in answering their questions, find normal conversation strange. Their most crying need is communication, so situations must be created where they can talk and ask questions.

'They need plenty of space so that they can run about and skip and enjoy themselves. They need to be able to shout and sing, which often they can't do at home, as father is in bed as he is on night shift. They need to hear good music at their own level. They need to be able to have the joy of moving to music, and so each school should have at least one good pianist as well as a gramophone, wireless and tape recorder. They need to be able to dress up as all generations of

160

children before them have done. This should lead naturally on to free drama among themselves, and not for an audience.'

Deprivation can take many guises. It can mean living in overcrowded conditions, being deafened by the noise of aeroplanes or constantly-passing trains, living in smoke-enshrouded communities or being brought up in a society to which the world of books, sophisticated conversation, peace and contemplation or the challenge of intellectual problems is foreign.

From *The Pre-School Years*, by Willem van der Eyken

Examples of Slum Neighbourhoods and Their Effects on People's Lives

A. LEEDS

Home may be private, but the front door opens out of the living-room on to the street, and when you go down the one step or use it as a seat on a warm evening you become part of the life of the neighbourhood.

To a visitor they are understandably depressing, these massed proletarian areas; street after regular street of shoddily uniform houses intersected by a dark pattern of ginnels and snickets (alleyways) and courts; mean, squalid, and in a permanent half-fog; a study in shades of dirty-grey, without greenness or the blueness of sky; degrees darker than the north or west of the town, than 'the better end'. The brickwork and the woodwork are cheap; the wood goes too long between repaintings – landlords are not as anxious to keep up the value of the property as are owner-occupiers. The nearest park or green open space is some distance away, but the terraces are gap-toothed with sour and brick-bespattered bits of wasteground and there is a piece of free ground half a mile away, called 't' Moor'. Evocative name: it is a clinkered six-acre stretch surrounded by works and grimy pubs, with a large red-brick urinal at its edge.

The houses are fitted into the dark and lowering canyons between the giant factories and the services which attend them: 'the barracks of an industry'. The goods-lines pass on embankments in and around, level with many of the bedroom windows, carrying the products of the men's work to South Africa, Nigeria, Australia. The viaducts interweave with the railway lines and with the canals below; the gas-works fit into a space somewhere between them all, and the pubs and graceless Methodist chapels stick up at intervals throughout. The green stuff of the region forces its way where it can – and that is almost everywhere – in stunted patches. Rough sooty grass pushes through the cobbles; dock and nettle insist on a defiant life in the rough and trampled earth-heaps at the corners of the waste-pieces, undeterred by 'dog-muck', cigarette packets, old ashes; rank elder, dirty privet, and rosebay willow-herb take hold in some of the 'backs' or in the walled-off space behind the Corporation Baths. All day and all night the noises and smells of the district – factory hooters, trains shunting, the stink of the gas-works – remind you that life is a matter of shifts and clockings-in-and-out. The children look improperly fed, inappropriately clothed, and as though they could do with more sunlight and green fields.

From *The Uses of Literacy*, by Richard Hoggart

B. NOTTINGHAM

St Ann's is a living area where the scarce trees stand as stunted hostages to rotting bricks and grey stones; where until recently there have been no play facilities for the children except the yards and streets, and where, during our investigation, a little boy was killed while playing on a derelict site. It is an area where the schools are old and decrepit; with dingy buildings and bleak factories and warehouses, functionally austere chapels, a host of second-hand shops stacked out with shabby, cast-off goods; overhung throughout the winter by a damp pall of smoke . . .

'In 1876 they built a school in St Ann's. Perhaps in those days it was an imposing building, with its tall neo-gothic windows. Now it is dirty and the soot-dampened rays of whatever sun gets through to St Ann's find it difficult to make their way to the children. The children, of course, are still there, packed in the warrened corridors and classrooms, or loosed into the minuscule play grounds which were scalloped out on two distinct and unconnectable levels. Eight or ten minutes' walk away is the nearest green patch, the one reception ground which serves the margins of St Ann's: and the top forms of the school have to crocodile down to the park in order to do their physical jerks, unless it rains or is too cold, in which case they are marched into the local Church Hall. It is a junior school, and rather than take the smallest children across busy main roads, they are exercised in the tiny playgrounds. The big kids are taken swimming in the Victoria Baths and to get there they have to be shepherded in a convoy for twenty minutes.

'This school contains ten useable classrooms, one of which has a sink, because it once passed as a biology laboratory at a time when the school also served to teach seniors. Through two classrooms there is an all-day stream of traffic to and from the cloakrooms, which are so situated as to cause the maximum social interaction, since they straddle the only entrance. Life is interesting for the teachers in these rooms, not only because of the processions which need to come and go through them, but also because of the noise that filters in from the playground while the first and second years are doing P.T. School dinners, until a year ago, were served in a dining centre, which involved another set of pilgrimages, across two hectic main roads. Now a small dining-room has been provided, and the children can be fed in two sittings. In the Assembly Hall it is hard to keep order because the room is too small to pack in the children in any civilized way. As is general in St Ann's the lavatories are out in the rain.'

What of the children who are put through these slum prisons? They are not well developed. They are on average smaller and less hardy than the middle-class kids from the suburbs. They don't win at the interschool games. They lack stamina, fall ill easily and are often absent from school. Every epidemic which hits the city booms in St Ann's. The school health service reports that fresh starters are often in need of attention for complaints which would ordinarily have been under care for some time. In one school a fifth of the children are treated each year for nits, as compared with just over a twentieth of the children at a school on a council estate, and none of the commuter-suburb school-children. They catch all sorts of other things, which are then shared around. Impetigo is common. They are not starving, but they frequently suffer from ill-balanced diets. Some of them come to school without breakfast, either because mother went off to work before them, or perhaps because the family got up late. A third of them get free school meals, as against a thirtieth of the children on the housing estate.

As many as two fifths of the school population investigated came from broken homes and 16 per cent were educationally subnormal. Eccentric behaviour was, not surprisingly, common in class.

A quarter of the children of St Ann's cannot read by the time they are seven: nearly half the seven-year-olds have reading ages of between four and five; a further third, between five and six; less than a tenth are average readers for their own age, and only 4 per cent are up to two years ahead of their peer-group. This compares with almost 60 per cent of the children aged seven in a commuter suburb on the outskirts of Nottingham, who had reading ages between one and five years in advance of the normal standards.

Children in Nottingham still go at 11 to either Grammar Schools or Second-ary Modern Schools. In the St Ann's area, the children make up only 1.5% of the Grammar School population, whereas in a residential suburb of Notting-ham, 60% of the children are given Grammar School places.

The Meadows (Another extensive Nottingham slum for which no rede-velopment plans exist)

90 per cent of the children were considered by their teachers to be to some extent emotionally disturbed; 65 per cent lived in homes in which their families shared accommodation with other families; 55 children out of 96 taking school meals received them free. To these figures should be added the teachers' impres-sions that probably all the children lived in substandard houses, that very many children lived in conditions of gross overcrowding, that many also lived in homes without high standards of cleanliness, in split families, in unstable houses, in unsettled families which moved house often or in homes which lacked books and in which parents did not take any great interest in the education of their children.

From *Poverty – The Forgotten Englishmen*, by Coates and Silburn

163

C. HULL

Terry Street is in an area of poor working class houses just off the Beverley Road in Hull. It is made up of terraces and back-to-back houses that were built during the last century. The people who live there are factory workers, unskilled and semi-skilled labourers. Here are two poems by Douglas Dunn about the people of Terry Street, but they could equally well apply to working class people living in the old houses in parts of your city.

NEW LIGHT ON TERRY STREET

First sunshine for three weeks, and the children came out
From their tents of chairs and old sheets,

Living room traffic jams, and battlefields of redcoat soldiers,
To expand, run with unsteady legs in and out of shades.

Up terraces of slums, young gum-chewing mothers sit
Outside on their thrones of light. Their radios,

Inside or placed on window ledges, grow hot
With sun and electricity. Shielding their eyes from sun

They talk above music, knitting or pushing prams
Over gentle, stone inches. Under the clawed chairs

Cats sleep in the furry shade. The children bounce balls
Up into their dreams of sand, and the sea they have not seen.

Becoming tired, the fascination of wheels takes them.
They pedal their trikes slowly through dust in hollows,

Quietly give up cheek to old men, sing with sly voices.
Their mothers go inside to cook. Their fathers come home.

Suddenly it is empty as life without the great ambition
Like living in a deep, dried-up riverbed, a throat that thirsts.

Yet there is no unrest. The dust is so fine.
You hardly notice you have grown too old to cry out for change.

YOUNG WOMEN IN ROLLERS

Because it's wet, the afternoon is quiet.
Children pacified with sweets inside
Their small houses, stroke travelling cats
From the kingdom of dustbins and warm smells.

Young women come to visit their married friends
Waiting for their hair to set beneath thin scarves,

Housing

They walk about in last year's fashions,
Stockingless, in coats and old shoes.

They look strong, white legged creatures
With nothing to do but talk of what it is to love
And sing the words softly to the new tunes.
The type who burst each other's blackheads

In the street and look in handbag mirrors
While they walk, not talking of the weather;
Who call across the street they're not wearing knickers,
But blush when they pass you alone.

This time they see me at my window, among books,
A specimen under glass, being protected,
And laugh at me watching them.
They minuet to Mozart playing loudly.

On the afternoon Third. They mock me thus,
They mime my softness. A landlord stares.
All he has worked for is being destroyed
The slum rent masters are at one with pop.

The movements they imagine go with minuet
Stay patterned on the air, I can see soot,
It floats. The whiteness of their legs has changed
Into something that floats, become like cloth.

They disappear into the house they come to visit.
Out of the open door rush last year's hits,
The music they listen to, that takes up their time
In houses that are monuments to entertainment.

I want to be touched by them, know their lives,
Dance in my own style, learn something new,
At night, I even dream of ideal communities
Why do they live where they live, the rich and the poor?

Tonight, when their hair is ready, after tea,
They'll slip through laws and the legs of policemen.
I won't be there, I'll be reading books elsewhere
There are many worlds, there are many laws.

Apathy
Slum houses with their overcrowding, damp, vermin, and poor sanitation

obviously affect the physical and mental health of their inhabitants. Deprived neighbourhoods lack space. Litter and rubbish is everywhere, the air is polluted, the surroundings depressing. In addition, one of the worst effects of poor environment is that the people become apathetic. They learn to take deprivation for granted, to put up with it and never expect anything better. This is how apathy is produced as this extract shows:

Human beings are almost infinitely adaptable, and provided that they are ill-treated consistently, they are apt to regard ill-treatment as 'natural'. If the lavatory leaks a little, and always has leaked a little, one comes to regard the leak as 'normal'. If the roof blows off such a lavatory, of course one will expect to be annoyed. But all the myriad petty discomforts can too easily be borne with remarkably little complaint. Damp, cold, rot, decrepitude are as 'natural' in St Ann's as is the smoky atmosphere: for all most people know, they have been sent by Providence and must be endured. Indeed, since Providence has never sent anything else, what other response would be possible? Only exceptional damp, unusual cold, excessive rot, and decrepitude to the point of collapse, are felt to be legitimate subjects of discussion. If you hang your washing out in the yard to dry, normally it will be attacked by numerous little black smuts: you will not normally complain. But when a particularly sulphurous bath of smuts burns holes in all your clothes while they are on the line, then you will complain. In the same way people mute their criticisms of what others would regard as intolerable housing amenities.

From *Poverty – The Forgotten Englishmen*, by Coates and Silburn

Discussion and Written Work

1 Describe as fully as you can from your own knowledge, and with the help of the passages above, the neighbourhood characteristics typical of a slum environment.

2(a) How does the health and physical development of slum children compare with that of middle class children in residential areas? Give specific examples from the passages to illustrate your answer.
(b) Why is the health of slum children poorer than average?
(c) Give examples from the passages to describe the homes and families of these children.
(d) What percentage of children in Britain come from environmentally-deprived homes?
(e) Show the ways in which a poor environment affects a child's educational ability and opportunity with reference to:

166

(i) talking
(ii) self-expression
(iii) reading
(iv) chance of grammar school entry

(f) Are working class children from slums always less intelligent than middle class children from the suburbs, or are there other reasons for their apparent lack of ability? Back up what you say by clear and detailed reasons.

3 Explain *in your own words* the feelings of the unknown hippy who wrote this poem:

SLUM SCHOOL (Hippy Song Anon.)

If the sons of company directors
And judges' private daughters
Had to go to school in a slum school
Dumped by some joker in a damp back alley,
Had to herd into classrooms cramped with worry
With a view onto slag heaps and stagnant pools
And play in a crackpot concrete cage.
Buttons would be pressed,
Rules would be broken,
Strings would be pulled
And magic words spoken,
Invisible fingers would mould
Palaces of gold.

4 Read again 'New Light on Terry Street'.
(a) Describe in your own words the games of the children in Terry Street.
(b) How do the young mothers spend their days in Terry Street, do you think? Give examples from the poem, but also use your own knowledge of life in a working class area.
(c) Explain carefully *in your own words* what is meant by:
(i) 'Suddenly it is empty as life without the great ambitions'.
(ii) 'You hardly notice you have grown too old to cry out for change.'

5 Read again 'Young Women in Rollers'.
(a) The poet and the young women live in the same street yet their ways of life are totally different:
(i) Give as many examples of the differences as you can from the poem.
(ii) Explain as fully as you can why their lives are different.

167

(b) Why do the young women behave differently to the poet depending on whether they are alone or in groups?

(c) Why does the poet call their houses 'monuments to entertainment'?

(d) What are the views, expressed in the last two verses, of the poet about his relationship with the young women?

6 Write a piece to describe what you think Terry Street must be like. (Make reference to: the types of houses; the day-to-day lives of the people – their interests, attitudes, and future prospects.)

7 Explain carefully why you think slum dwellers are often apathetic.

8 Find out all you can about the organisation Shelter – you can get information from their London Headquarters at 86, The Strand, London, WC2R OEQ – then find out the following:

(a) What does the Shelter organisation hope to achieve?

(b) What methods does Shelter use to further its aims and to publicise its activities?

(c) What is a Housing Association?

(d) Find out what are the difficulties facing Shelter, and give your own views on them.

(e) How successful has Shelter been in improving the housing situation in this country?

(If there is a Shelter group in your area you could arrange for a speaker to come to talk to you; perhaps you will be able to help.)

Unit 3. Slum Clearance and Redevelopment

The clearing of slum neighbourhoods is accepted as an important priority by most local authorities. Some build new houses in the cleared areas, others fringe their cities with new housing estates into which the one-time slum dwellers are moved.

You can often read in the newspaper about people, and in particular old people, who are very sad to see the neighbourhood in which they have spent most of their lives destroyed. Some even refuse to leave and squat stubbornly in their homes while the demolition men pull the houses apart around them. In the end, of course, they have no alternative but to go. Many are moved into pensioners' bungalows on new estates or into Old Folks' Homes. Some are rehoused locally in accommodation not yet scheduled for demolition, as this account shows:

He had an acre of space to himself and it was all condemned and useless. Time had worn the front step so that the door hung clear of the step and the knocker, after a thousand hammerings, had etched its plan into the wood. Where the boss of the knocker hit there was a hole. Behind was the wasteland where they were re-building and you stood with your back to it and bashed on the door and the wind came up and cut into you and into the house.

You knew he was in because the door was bolted at the bottom and you kicked it to make sure it was so and then you hammered again and shouted through the letter-box and perhaps he would come and perhaps he would not.

Newspapers were piled high in the passage way and you edged past them to follow him up the stairs to his two rooms high up at the back of the house. His bed was a nest of rags. There was a gas-ring and gas lighting and an old cast-iron grate with no coal in it. Over the end of the bed was his one decent pair of trousers.

He started as a boy on the Pullman coaches and earned 5s per week but you couldn't find out all the details of his life as his mind 'goes away now and again'. He was 73 years old and tough and wore hedgers' gloves against the cold. The Council had wanted to rehouse him but he was stubborn and would not move away from his Church. We knew that if the cold went on he would take to his bed and it would be too much trouble for him to get up and eat.

We badgered the Council to provide for him a place he would accept. It was not a bad winter but the cold and the wind seemed endless. As it lasted so our guilt grew. What we could do for him was inadequate. Perhaps once or twice a week we got to see him and at the week-ends we sometimes saw his son.

No one liked him. He had a good job and a car and a Council flat for which he wasn't paying much money and he played badminton to keep himself in trim. He had no room in his flat in which to put his father, he said, and he had told him 'quite frankly' that if he did not move out he would die.

Well, the old man survived the winter, then, one spring day, he was moved by the Council into a basement flat that was huge and old and clean and re-decorated so that he still had an acre of space to himself. It was just a better sort of space.

We helped the old man with his moving and got rid of the filthy bed. There were not enough volunteers to do all the work we wanted to do and so our visits to him slacked but he was still 'our old man' and we still thought of him. He couldn't manage his housework so we arranged with the Local Authority for a home help to visit him.

Some of us concede that, some of the time, the Council knows what it's doing. But all of us know that, if it hadn't been for our warm, angry, unprofessional, non-prying Service, a cantankerous old man, who started on the Pullmans at five bob a week would not now be living, by himself, near his Church, in an acre of warm space.

'Help' 12 – Arthur Jacklin

A New Environment

For many people slum clearance and rehousing means a change of environment and leaving a neighbourhood which many have grown up in and even, in a strange sort of way, have become attached to. Here are three accounts of moving house:

A. *A REMOVAL FROM TERRY STREET*

On a squeaking cart, they push the usual stuff,
A mattress, bed ends, cups, carpets, chairs,
Four paperback westerns. Two whistling youths
In surplus U.S. Army battle-jackets
Remove their sister's goods. Her husband
Follows, carrying on his shoulders the son
Whose mischief we are glad to see removed,
And pushing, of all things, a lawnmower.
There is no grass in Terry Street. The worms
Come up cracks in concrete yards in moonlight.
That man, I wish him well. I wish him grass.

Douglas Dunn

B. GREENLEIGH

Less than twenty miles away from Bethnal Green, the automatic doors of the tube train open on to the new land of Greenleigh. On one side of the railway are cows at pasture. On the other, the new housing estate. Instead of the shops of Bethnal Green there is the shopping centre at the Parade; instead of the street barrows piled high with fruit, fish and dresses, instead of the cries of the costermongers from Spitalfields to Old Ford, there are orderly self-service stores in the marble halls of the great combines. In place of the gaunt buildings rising above narrow streets of narrow houses, there are up-to-date semi-detached residences. Bethnal Green encases the history of three hundred years. Cottages built for the descendants of Huguenot refugees, with their wide weavers' windows and peeling plaster, stand next to Victorian red-brick on one side and massive blocks of Edwardian charity on the other. Greenleigh belongs firmly to the aesthetics of this mid-century. Built since the war to a single plan, it is all of one piece. Though the Council has mixed different types of houses, row upon row look practically identical, each beside a concrete road, each enclosed by a fence, each with its little patch of flower garden at front and larger patch of vegetable garden at back, each with expansive front windows covered over with net curtains; all built, owned, and guarded by a single responsible landlord.

Instead of the hundred fussy, fading little pubs of the borough, there are just the neon lights and armchairs of the Merchant Venturer and the Yeoman Arms. Instead of the barrel organ in Bethnal Green Road there is an electrically amplified musical box in a mechanical ice-cream van. In place of tiny workshops squeezed into a thousand backyards rise the first few glass and concrete factories which will soon give work to Greenleigh's children. Instead of the sociable squash of people and houses, workshops and lorries, there are the drawn-out roads and spacious open ground of the usual low-density estate. Instead of the flat land of East London, the gentle hills of Essex.

From *Family and Kinship in East London*, by Willmott and Young

C. STEPHEN REHOUSED

Six-year-old Stephen is a lively red head that I met recently. The house was newly painted and when I rang the bell Stephen's mother answered and invited me in.

Stephen rushed up to me, grabbed me by the hand. 'We've got a bathroom, look', he laughed. 'Look this is my room. Come and look at the toilet. Mum's got a kitchen.'

This was Stephen's first real 'home'. He, mother and sister had been one of Britain's three million families living in slums, or in slum-like and overcrowded conditions. They had no bathroom, shared a toilet, and Mum's 'kitchen' was a corner of the one damp room they shared at the top of a West London house. The bed in which they all slept was in the other corner. Eventually Mum faced up to the fact that the conditions were affecting Stephen's health, both physically and mentally, and had sadly allowed him to be taken into a children's home. There he was one of the 5,000 children 'in care' because their parents are living in unsatisfactory home conditions.

Later, relations took him into their home and he became one of the thousands of children living with parents and friends – because their parents had unsatisfactory living accommodation. Happily the family never became completely 'homeless'. They never became one of the 12,500 people living in a hostel for the homeless. Now they live in a two roomed flat with kitchen and bathroom.

'Shelter' reporter

The Social Effects of Moving House

Moving to a new house from the slums is more than merely getting to know a new environment; it is often the beginning of a new way of life, as these two extracts show:

A. GREENLEIGH

The people of Bethnal Green in moving to Greenleigh 'left two or three damp rooms built in the last century for the "industrious classes" and were suddenly transported to a spacious modern home. Instead of the tap in the backyard, there is a bathroom with hot and cold water. Instead of the gas stove on the landing, a real kitchen with a sink and a larder. Instead of the narrow living room with stained wallpaper and shaky floorboards, a newly painted lounge heated by a modern solid fuel grate. And instead of the street for their children to play in, fields and trees and open country.'

The house when the builders leave it is only a shell. The house when people move into it comes to life. They bestow an authority upon it, even vest it with a kind of personality: up to a point it then decrees what they shall do within its walls. The house is also a challenge, demanding that their style of life shall accord with the standard it sets. When they make a first cup of tea after the removal van has driven away and look around their mansion, they are conscious not only of all they have got which they never had before but also of all the things they need which they still lack. The furniture brought from Bethnal Green looks old and forlorn against the bright paint. They need carpets for the lounge, lino for the stairs, and mats for the front door. They need curtains. They need another bed. They need a kitchen table. They need new lampshades, pots and pans, grass seed and spades, clothes lines and bath mats, Airwick and Jeyes, mops and pails – all the paraphernalia of modern life for a house two or three times larger and a hundred times grander than the one they left behind them. With the aid of their belongings, they need somehow to live the kind of life, be the kind of people, that will fit into Forest Close or Cambridge Avenue. Then they, and the house, can at last be comfortable. They have to acquire new property. They have to acquire new habits.

The first essential is money for material possessions.When people move to Greenleigh the standard of life, measured by the quality of housing, is at once raised. They attempt to bring the level in other respects up to the same standard. Furniture and carpets have to be bought, and although, with the aid of hire purchase, this can be done without capital, it cannot be done without a burden on income. Moreover, the house is only the beginning. A nice house and shabby clothes, a neat garden and an old box of a pram, do not go together. 'My sister

172

gave me a beautiful Dunkley pram,' said Mrs Berry, 'because I was going to such a beautiful new house.' Smartness calls for smartness.

This understandable urge to acquisition can easily become competitive. People struggle to raise their all-round standards to those of the home, and in the course of doing so, they look for guidance to their neighbours. To begin with, the first-comers have to make their own way. The later arrivals have their model at hand. The neighbours have put up nice curtains. Have we? They have got their garden planted with privet and new grass-seed. Have we? They have a lawn-mower and a Dunkley pram. What have we got? The new arrivals watch the first-comers, and the first-comers watch the new arrivals. All being under the same pressure for material advance, they naturally mark each other's progress. Those who make the most progress are those who have proved their claim to respectability, Greenleigh-style. The fact that people are watching their neighbours and their neighbours watching them provides the further stimulus, reinforcing the process set in motion by the new house, to conform to the norms of the estate.

From Family and Kinship in East London, by Willmott and Young

B. WESTWOOD

(When Kevin Thompson left the East End of London and moved to West-wood Estate, his family faced exactly this kind of situation.)

We looked up at our square brick house, with its bay window and its new paint-work, as respectable as anything.

'Oh, isn't it *lovely*!' said Sandra again.

'Lovely?' said Walter. 'Thirty shillin's a week rent to pay, instead o' ten! Two miles to t'pub and twelve miles to work. Lovely?'

'It's a sight better than that 'ole we've come from,' said Doris.

'Well, you better not start complainin' about it, anyroad,' said Walter. 'It was you that wanted to come 'ere, not me, an' don't you forget it.'

'We 'adn't no option that I can see,' said Doris. 'We couldn't 'ave stayed on in a tent when they pulled t'house down, could we?'

Meanwhile Walter, inside the house, issued instructions to the rest of us, and Sandra and I got on with the work, not taking much notice. It wasn't until the job was finished that Doris came inside. She looked first at the living-room, then at the kitchen.

'It dun't look much, does it?' she said.

I knew just what she meant. The truth was that our furniture was nothing but a few sticks. There were just enough chairs to go round, but most of them were rickety. There was a decrepit old table and a dresser with a cracked marble top and a broken-down sofa and a few other oddments, and that was all we had downstairs. Upstairs was no better. In Orchard Grove it hadn't seemed to matter, because the house was so old and poky and dirty that proper furniture would be wasted on it. But here in the nice new council house our few bits and pieces looked very poor.

'It's what you 'ad before,' said Walter.

'Well it won't do 'ere,' said Doris.

'Gettin' to be quite the 'ousewife, eh?' said Walter jeeringly. 'I never 'eard you say owt about furniture at Orchid Grove. You'll be wantin' carpets next, I suppose, an' tablecloths. Goin' up in t'world. Maybe you think you'll 'ave Lord an' Lady Tomnoddy droppin' in for a cup o' tea now you're in Westwood. "Can I press you to a jam tart, my lady?" Aw, come off it, can't you?'

'There'd be money to buy summat decent if only you stopped spendin' all your wages on beer an' 'orses.'

Walter flared up.

'It's nowt to do wi' you how I spend my wages. I earn them, don't I?'

From *Widdershins Crescent*, by John Rowe Townsend

Multi-Storey Flats

For many people, re-housing is in multi-storey flats.

A survey about young children between two and five years old living in high flats showed that 72% living above the third storey only rarely played with other children of their own age because no safe-play opportunities had been provided for them.

In the old housing areas, the street was the child's playground, providing opportunities for discovery and adventure, but at a high price. In one half of a square mile of North Kensington a child is hit by a car every five days. Others end up in juvenile court after their play has got out of hand. Mother and child may have to go some way to find a public garden or park. In high flats on new estates there are no streets. The open spaces are often meaningless and empty, the grass frequently fenced off and prohibited. If the toddler is lucky, there may be a play area designed for his age group. If he is very lucky, there will be sand and water to play with. For the mothers there may be seats where they can sit together and chat while their children play. But the architects who built their homes ignored the fact that families have children. A special place for play in the home is as essential as a room for eating and sleeping. Young mothers confined to the flat with two or three small children, lifts and stairs, and little space to play can quickly become tired and depressed.

For older children the builders' rubble of half-completed houses provides an adventure playground with countless attractions. But when 'discovery' becomes 'trespass' and 'high spirits' become 'damage to property', then these children can find themselves in trouble again. Youth clubs and recreational facilities are frequently the last amenities to be provided on new estates, the very areas which usually have a higher than average proportion of youngsters. Often living well away from the neighbourhoods they know and at a distance from the city-centres of entertainment, young people on new housing estates are notoriously 'at a loose end' and looking for something to do.

The alternative to new housing estates is often to clear the slums and build afresh in their place. In Stepney, tower blocks spring up where terrace cottages once crouched.

Trevor Huddleston is Bishop of Stepney, where it takes eight years to persuade the council to turn a rubbish dump into a playground. He says:

Look out of my window. The lorries thunder down to the docks and children wait interminably to cross from one side of the road to another. Look at this street. You can't see the earth. It doesn't exist for the people who live here. There is no earth, there's just concrete and asphalt and bricks and mortar. There's not a living thing!

There is development taking place everywhere in the East End, and it has gone ahead without considering the element of community. Where there might have been shopping precincts with a church and recreation centre, enough people to fill a small town find themselves with no assembly point and no means of contact. In the old days, a poor street of houses was a community. Every door latch had a string attached to it so that if anyone wasn't seen at the front door for a few hours, people could go in and see what had happened. How do you do that in a 19-storey block housing thousands of people? How can you create community in a broiler house?

The image of living like chickens in a broiler house or hens in a battery has frequently been used to describe the packing of multi-storey flats with people, as this poem by Edwin Brock shows:

SONG OF THE BATTERY HEN

We can't grumble about accommodation:
We have a new concrete floor that's
always dry, four walls that are
painted white, and a sheet iron roof
the rain drums on. A fan blows warm air
beneath our feet to disperse the smell
of chicken shit and, on dull days,
fluorescent lighting sees us.

You can tell me: if you come by
the north door, I am in the twelfth pen

on the left hand side of the third row
from the floor; and in that pen
I am usually the middle one of three.
But, even without directions, you'd
discover me. I have the same orange-
red comb, yellow beak and auburn
feathers, but as the door opens and you
hear above the electric fan a kind of
one word wail, I am the one
who sounds loudest in my head.

Listen. Outside this house there's an
orchard with small moss green apple
trees; beyond that, two fields of
cabbages; then on the far side of
the road, a broiler house. Listen;
one cockerel crows out there, as
tall and proud as the first hour of sun.
Sometimes I stop calling with the others
to listen, and wonder if he hears me.

The next time you come here, look for me.
Notice the way I sound inside my head.
God made us all quite differently,
and blessed us with this expensive home.

When you have considered the living conditions of a battery hen, think about the ways in which Edwin Brock's observations could equally well be applied to humans in multi-storey flats. Here are some:

(a) 'We can't grumble about accommodation.' The modern flats are newly built and well equipped compared with the slums. They are weather-proof, where the slums had let in wind and rain, brightly lit and frequently centrally heated.

(b) 'I am in the twelfth pen on the left hand side of the third row from the floor.' Flats provide at regular intervals identical accommodation of floors and window space for hundreds of people. From the outside each little living cell looks exactly the same as all the others.

(c) 'I am the one who sounds loudest in my head.' The people themselves may all appear to be much the same and even to look alike as their environment moulds them into a common pattern, but each is an individual in his own right and important to himself.

(d) 'Outside this house there's an orchard with small moss green apple trees: beyond that, two fields of cabbages. . . .' Outside the living block there is a

176

world of air and freedom and nature to be enjoyed if only it can be reached. But across the road is another broiler house, another block of multi-storey flats, each identical to the next and packed with similar people. Do they ever think or wonder about each other?

(e) *'Look for me. Notice the way I sound inside my head. God made us all quite differently and blessed us with this expensive home.'* Rehoused from the slums in bright new flats, the people should be content and able to persuade themselves that they are happy. But they face now the depression caused by conformity, the loss of individuality, the feeling of isolation, and the need for human contact. What they need is to be noticed and to be looked-out for by friendly faces.

Suburbia

Suburbia is the area of housing on the fringes of towns and cities where there are no factories and where the neighbourhood is cleaner, more spacious, and pleasantly near to the countryside. The houses are either on small private estates or suburban roads: self-contained, privately owned, and separated from neighbours by carefully tended gardens. These are the homes of the middle classes who want peace and privacy, who enjoy a much better standard of living than the slum dwellers, and whose work and leisure activities contrast significantly with those of council estate dwellers. In an age which is supposed to represent a classless Britain, we cannot deny the fact that housing divisions are one of the main ways of disproving this supposition.

Town Planning

Mother
there's a block of flats going up in the bedroom,
a carpark in the lounge
it's a sin
They're building a town centre in the toilet,
what a shocking estate
we are in.

Roger McGough

The towns and cities which sprang up in the nineteenth century with the Industrial Revolution rambled and spread without much thought or planning. Today eight out of every ten people in Britain live in towns and cities, and the numbers are growing. The mistakes of the last hundred and fifty years have now been realised, however, and much more careful thought is given to town planning by specially trained experts.

177

In the process of planning, sociologists play an important part because they have investigated the effects of environment on people's lives and can offer advice based on detailed research to the town planners. Evidence of stress caused by living in multi-storey flats has persuaded many local authorities to cut them out of their future housing schemes.

The loss of community and the loneliness caused by moving people from slums and to impersonal new estates has been reduced in many cities by moving people, streets and terraces at a time into the same neighbourhood units on the estates. The long rows of identical houses favoured by post-War builders have given way to little squares, courts, and closes where community feelings can flourish. The evidence of the vandalism of restless youth has been used to persuade councils to provide clubs, community centres, and recreation facilities on new estates and to build them at the same time as the houses, rather than much later, if at all. In these ways planners have learned valuable lessons from sociological investigations.

Some re-housing schemes have been more ambitious and whole new towns have been built in the country to take the overspill population from already-crowded cities. In 1946 a New Towns Act was passed providing for the development of 23 new towns to add to the few garden cities which had been built before the War. Some of the most exciting experiments in planning have taken place in these new towns to try to improve the general quality of the environment in which people live.

All the housing problems are by no means solved, however; the slums are still with us and many people argue that badly planned redevelopment schemes are already creating the modern slums of the future. The housing question has been likened to a political football, kicked around by politicians at election time but then conveniently forgotten once the season is over.

Discussion and Written Work

1 Why are some people reluctant to leave their old houses, even though these are in slum areas?

2 Describe some of the changes in living conditions and environment experienced by slum dwellers who have been re-housed.

3 Why is moving house from the slums to a new estate not just a change of address but the beginning of a new way of life?

4 In what ways are the new estate dwellers persuaded to improve their standard of living?

5 From what you know about the development of home-centredness on estates, how do you think Walter's attitudes and behaviour in Westwood might change?

6 (a) Make a summary of all the arguments expressed in the passages which criticise tower blocks of flats in redevelopment areas and new estates.
(b) Add any further criticisms you can make from your own knowledge.
(c) Write an essay entitled, 'In Defence of the Multi-Storeys', which presents as many well argued points as possible to illustrate the better side of such accommodation.

7 (a) Is there much evidence of new housing development in your city? How well planned are the new estates?
(b) Are there recreational facilities and sufficient amenities for the residents?
(c) Is there much evidence of vandalism? How can you account for this?
(d) What proportion of people still live in delapidated areas? Are these areas scheduled for redevelopment in the near future?
    (Perhaps you could arrange a visit from a local councillor or member of the Town Planning Office to help you to answer some of your questions.)

Class Project: Social Class Housing Divisions
You can test the social class divisions in your own city. Arrange in a small group to visit both a working class street in an old part of town or a council housing estate *and* a middle class suburban road.
    What do you notice about the houses and the neighbourhood?

A. QUESTIONNAIRE TO HOUSEHOLDERS
(Explain to householders on first meeting: We are from ——————— school and we are conducting a survey about housing as part of our studies. We should like to ask you a few questions about your household, if it is convenient.)

1 What is the occupation of the male head of your household?
2 (a) Does the wife in your household go out to work?
   (b) (*If Yes*) Is her occupation full-time or part-time? What job does she do?
3 (a) Could you please tell us the number of children in your family?
   (b) Do you have any children in the 11–15 age group? (State how many) Which school(s) do they attend?
   (c) Do you have any children in the 15–18 age group? (State how many) Are they still at school?
       Did they leave school at 15?

Did they leave school between 16–17?

Did they leave school at 18?

(d) (i) Have you any children who have left school? (State how many)

    (ii) If you have any children who have left school, could you please tell us what they did when they left:

        (a) name of occupation?

        (b) type of further education?

4 (a) Do you have a cleaning lady to help you in the house?

  (b) Do you have a telephone?

  (c) Do you have a motor car?

  (d) Do you have your own garage?

  (e) (i) Have you been on holiday during the last year?

     (ii) May we ask you where you spent your holiday?

  (f) How long have you been living in this house?

Thank you very much for your help in answering our questions.

B. INTERPRETING YOUR FINDINGS

When all your questionnaires have been completed, sort out the findings of the class as a whole.

1 What was the total number of houses visited:

(a) in a street in an old part of town?

(b) in a council estate?

(c) in a suburban road?

2(a) Study the occupations of your male householders and classify them into the following groups:

    (i) Lower working class (Unskilled and semi-skilled trades, manual)

    (ii) Upper working class (Clerical and skilled trades)

    (iii) Lower middle class (White collar, small business, lesser professional)

    (iv) Upper middle class (Professional, managerial and wealthy business-men)

(Ask your teacher about the jobs you are not sure how to classify.)

(b) What proportion of each social class live in each of the areas visited?

(c) Write a detailed description of the type of work usually done by suburban dwellers compared to the type of work usually done by estate or 'old street' dwellers.

3(a) What percentage of women went out to work in:

    (i) a street in an old part of town?

    (ii) a council estate?

    (iii) a suburban road?

(b) Write a paragraph to compare the types of jobs done by the three categories of women.

4(a) Work out the average number of children in:
    (i) an 'old street' family
    (ii) an estate family
    (iii) a suburban road family
(b) Write a piece to compare the typical school experience of children from these families, commenting on types of schools attended and the ages at which they left.
(c) What percentage of the children who had left school went on to further education from:
    (i) the 'old street' families?
    (ii) the 'estate' families?
    (iii) the suburban road families?
(d) Compare the occupations of the children in the three categories in (c) above who had left school and not gone on to further education.
5 What percentage in each of the three categories had:
(a) cleaning help in the house?
(b) a telephone?
(c) a car?
(d) a garage?
6 What percentage of families in each of the three categories:
(a) did not go away on holiday?
(b) holidayed near to home (within a radius of 60 miles)?
(c) went abroad for their holidays?
7 What is significant about the length of time during which the various families had been living in their houses? (Give reasons for what you say, and add your own comments.)
8 When the findings of the class as a whole have been interpreted and all the statistics have been collected, use this information to show the different social class compositions of suburban roads, streets in the old areas of town, and council estates.

Acknowledgements

The Author and Hutchinson Educational are grateful to the following for their permission to reproduce copyright material: Mrs. Ellen Wright and Jonathan Cape Ltd: *Black Boy* by Richard Wright; Richard Hoggart and Chatto & Windus: *The Uses of Literacy* by Richard Hoggart; Collier-Macmillan, New York: *Human Society* by Kinsley Davis; Collins: *The African Child* by Camara Laye; Curtis Brown Ltd: *Growing up in New Guinea* by Margaret Mead; Faber and Faber Ltd: *Married Life in New Guinea* by Isaac Schapera; Michael Joseph Ltd: *The Fire Next Time* by James Baldwin, *A Kestrel for A Knave* by Barry Hines; Victor Gollancz Ltd: *Male and Female* by Margaret Mead, *New Lives for Old* by Margaret Mead; Granada Publishing Ltd: *The Fishermen* by J. Tunstall; William Heinemann Ltd: *Report from a Chinese Village* by Jan Myrdal; David Higham Associates Ltd and Jonathan Cape Ltd: *The Soul of the Ape* by Eugene Marais; The Hogarth Press Ltd: *The Lost World of the Kalihari* and *The Heart of the Hunter* by Laurens van der Post; Holt Rinehart and Winston Inc: *Tepoztlán: Village in Mexico* by Oscar Lewis; Hutchinson: *The Unknown Citizen* by Tony Parker and *Widdershins Crescent* by J. R. Townsend; Inter-Varsity Press and Tyndale Press: *The World's Religions* (Third Edition) Ed. Anderson; Longman Group Ltd: *The Arabian Sands* and *The Marsh Arabs* by Wilfred Thesiger, *The Status Seekers* by Vance Packard; Mental Health Trust and Research Fund: 'Problems of Old Age' (Pamphlet No. 4); *New Society*: 'The Seven Ages of Man' by Anthony Ambrose; Penguin Books Ltd: *Breaking The Silence* © W. J. Weatherby 1965, *Work: Twenty Personal Accounts* and *Work 2* by Ronald Fraser, *Invitation to Sociology* by Peter Berger, *The Unattached* by Mary Morse, *Poverty: The Forgotten Englishman* by Kenneth Coates and Richard Silburn, *Child Care and the Growth of Love* by John Bowlby, *The Pre-School Years* by William van der Eyken, *Young Teachers and Reluctant Learners* by Charles Hannam, Norman Stephenson and Pat Smyth; Laurence Pollinger Ltd: *Coming of Age in Samoa* by Margaret Mead, *The Feminine Mystique* by Betty Friedan; Routledge & Kegan Paul Ltd: *Adolescent Boys of East London* by Peter Willmott and *Family and Kinship in East London* by Michael Young and Peter Willmott, *The Captive Wife* by Hannah Gavron, *Education and the Working Class* by Brian Jackson and Dennis Marsden, *The Family Life of Old People* by Peter Townsend; Martin Secker & Warburg Ltd: *Children of Sanchez* by Oscar Lewis.

Every effort has been made to ensure accurate acknowledgement. The Publishers would be glad to know of any corrections for subsequent reprints.

Index

Index

Index